Only Originals

TALES OF OUTSTANDING UNRESTORED CARS

©2009 Krause Publications, Inc., a subsidiary of F+W Media, Inc.

Published by

700 East State Street • Iola, WI 54990-0001
715-445-2214 • 888-457-2873
www.krausebooks.com

Our toll-free number to place an order or obtain
a free catalog is (800) 258-0929.

Library of Congress Control Number: 2009939599

ISBN-13: 978-1-4402-1378-6
ISBN-10: 1-4402-1378-X

Designed by Sharon Bartsch
Edited by Brian Earnest

Printed in the United States of America

CONTENTS

By Angelo Van Bogart

THE AIR OF AN ORIGINAL

Rain, snow, sleet, hail and intense sun are just the beginning of the instruments of torture Mother Nature can use to beat up an automobile or truck. Some vehicles hold up admirably under these circumstances, coming through the abuses with nary a ding or rust spot, thanks to fine engineering, cautious caretakers and simple good fortune. Other vehicles fail miserably, winding up in a wrecker's clutches, forgotten in a farmer's field or even at the bottom of a lake. A fortunate few avoid the elements and rigors of human use altogether, and after a score or more years have passed, they remain factory fresh.

Given the amount of time and miles that can pass and the limitless circumstances that can affect a vehicle's condition, it's rare to find a collectible vehicle in fine, original condition. Such well-preserved vehicles have always been treasured in the old car hobby, whether it be as good "driver" cars, possible projects for "better than new" restorations or show vehicles that are displayed on their own merits. More than ever, excellent originals are being treasured for what they are: Excellent examples of how it was. These cars can educate the restorer of a similar car, yet with their minor flaws from the passage of time, be driven and shown, and appreciated by acute collectors.

When it comes to determining what constitutes an original, the *Old Cars Weekly* staff's criteria requires a vehicle to retain more than 50 percent original features in each of the following categories: paint, interior, chrome and other bright work and mechanical parts (with provisions acceptable to keep a vehicle safely operating). Modifications must be minimal and limited to the period in which the vehicle was manufactured. All of the vehicles in this book meet these standards.

There are several clubs and events that honor unrestored vehicles, notably the Antique Automobile Club of America through its Historic Preservation of Original Features class of judging; the Pebble Beach Concours d'Elegance's unrestored class; and Bloomington Gold events — gatherings that were once limited to Chevrolet Corvettes, but recently began incorporating unrestored collector cars of all varieties to participate in Bloomington Gold's respected Survivor category of judging.

Unrestored originals have long been cherished by the *Old Cars Weekly* staff, and some of our favorites from the publication's pages and readers' exceptional garages are included in this book. Our staff thanks those readers for appreciating these cars, and for sharing them with others.

Story and photos by Gerald Perschbacher

THE HUNT FOR AN ORIGINAL

Trying to pick out the right unrestored car can be a delightful challenge

This 1940 Packard Super Eight is a nice original car
that displays plenty of evidence of pampering. One of
the telltale spots is the running board step area by the
driver's door. Generally, if this spot is in nice shape,
the owner was being careful with the rest of the car.

It's been decided. You want an old, original, unrestored car. As you begin the search, you wonder what to note in a candidate, what to expect once you buy it, and how you can preserve what's there.

After you have found a possible candidate, verify the authenticity of the vehicle in your first contact with the seller. If contact is made via e-mail, ask for pictures, especially close-ups. But realize that visuals

The instrument panel is a good barometer for a car's condition. Also, check closely for cracks or warps in the steering wheel that detract from the car's beauty and affect driving.

can be deceptive. Tiny scratches or buffing swirls in paint may not be seen clearly.

If you make contact by phone or e-mail, ask about the car's history. Where was it sold new? Who owned it (and who subsequently owned it)? How long was it owned by those people? Was anything changed from original? How is the paint — is it dull or with full luster, are there thin spots showing primer? Is there rust anywhere? Any evidence of an accident over the years? If so, what was damaged or replaced?

If the car was a luxury vehicle, such as a limousine, it may have had a chauffeur. If so, good for you. This usually means the car was broken in properly and was care-

fully serviced during its early years. However, even the nicest luxury car was usually sold within 10-15 years. Many went to large families, and interiors received a beating in subsequent normal use.

Open cars can be prone to floor rust. If there is wood construction in the car, make sure the wood is solid. You may buy a fine-looking original car that has been hit by termites, dry rot or other problems. A major hidden flaw can make your new purchase a nightmare.

Let's examine the points surrounding a 1940 Packard Super Eight — a fine, low-mileage car.

No wood construction was used on 1940

To be considered an "original," a car still has to have its factory upholstery. Pay particular attention to wooden pieces, and also look closely to see how much the fabrics used inside have faded over time.

Packards, but senior models from 1939 on back used a heavy amount of wood. So did many other carmakers, regardless of price class. Consult an expert or check print sources to determine if wood is an issue.

Exterior examination

Walk up front and examine the car. Is the paint shiny and lively in appearance? If it is slightly dull, ask permission to gently rub an obscure section with your clean hand or, even better, ask if the seller could polish a small section to see how it will shine. How is the fit of the hood? Examine brightwork and the hood mascot (ornament or Moto-Meter),

watching for pits, scratches, rust and loose areas. Do hood handles and latches work fine? Are any parts broken or missing? Either make mental notes or use a small pad of paper to write a list of strengths and weaknesses as you study the car's condition.

Pay special attention to the front trim, since this was often prone to imperfections caused by normal driving. Since cars commonly were pushed when they failed to start or were bumped in parking areas, examine front and rear bumpers for damage. If the car has thermostatically controlled shutters in its grille, check for operation. Shutters should automatically close when the engine is cool,

then open as it heats in operation. If the shutters are jammed open to allow continuous cooling, don't consider it a problem you cannot fix, but realize it before you buy.

Check glass lenses for cracks. Watch for thin spots in the paint, especially on top ridges of fenders which seemed prone to heavier polishing over the years. If the car carries side-mounted spare tires with covers, check that the tires are there — at least the original wheel rims — and that the covers are intact and in good condition.

Running boards, whether hidden or exposed, should be rust-free and in good condition. Carefully inspect the support brackets underneath. Of equally prime importance is the condition of the running board covering. Cars from the 1920s and earlier often used linoleum. In the 1930s and early 1940s, this gave way to rubber. One of the first areas to show wear is the rubber. Examine the step area by the driver's door. If this is in excellent condition, then the car probably was pampered. Test the liveliness of the rubber. If you ever need to repair or replace the rubber, find out your options from specialty companies dealing with rubber for old cars. There are also products that can liven old rubber. Check with various companies that deal with rubber issues regularly.

Interior motives

Give the interior close scrutiny. Is everything entirely authentic? Note any degree of fading by finding a portion of the material that was not exposed to bright sunlight. If you can, press against the seat and back cushions to determine if the underlying stuffing and supports are OK. Be extremely observant for holes and stains left by insects and mice. Take note of any odors that might signal musty dampness or other problems.

Cars in the 1950s popularized the use of foam rubber in seat cushions. The material disintegrates with time and temperature, so check the floor under the front seat to see if there is a white or yellowish dust on the floor. If there is, then the foam rubber is falling apart and should be replaced. The good news is that this may be done in many cases without damaging the good upholstery and without cosmetically changing the originality.

In the case of certain luxury cars in the early 1940s, duck or goose feathers were used for the stuffing. If you find a loose feather floating around now and then, it's not a big problem. It just means there is a slight tear in the never-seen underlining. However, if there is a big pile of feathers, then find the hidden problem and repair it.

The instrument panel is a good barometer for a car's condition. See if it shows signs of being sun-beaten near the windshield. Note any change in texture, shine or general condition. Plastic and bakelite became the miracle material for decorative dash accents at this time. The more that was used, the more expensive the automobile, so it seemed. That's because the use of plastic was very costly at first and it allowed for wide artistic expression.

Be sensitive to cracks or warps in the steering wheel that distract from the car's beauty and affect driving. Count all knobs and switches and examine their condition. It might not be too difficult to find a new-old-stock or slightly used replacement.

Some trunk compartments were fully carpeted. Don't hesitate to open the trunk and peruse its condition. Ask about the items inside to make sure what will go with the car, should you buy it. Expect a bumper jack. Sometimes there are tools and a tool bag. Lucky is the buyer who finds documents from the car's initial sale. An owner's manual in good condition is always a pleasant find.

Trunks were prone to leakage and undercarpet rust. Be wary. Also check the fit of the trunk lid and how well its support holds it up. While at the back, examine the tail lamps and lenses.

Once you have made close examination, step back and get the whole picture. Open doors and watch for sagging at the hinges.

Review for repairs

Look for old body repairs, repainted areas, dents and dings, rust along the lower edge of doors and fenders and problems with the roof. Too many cars have had something fall on their tops, causing dents or impressions. Many times, judges don't find these at a car show unless they are major. But since you will be living with the car, know what it offers before you buy.

Once you see body welds or fender welts, cautiously eye them for possible problems. If welting has been buffed away, is loose or even missing, it can detract from the overall appearance.

Chassis check

Spend a good amount of time under the chassis with a bright flash light, observing leaks, rust, cracks, strange repairs, etc. Look throughout the engine compartment with a fine eye. Be sure to start the car and examine the tail pipe for smoke, listen closely for strange noises and take the car for a drive before you buy. If possible, bring a friend with you who knows the mechanical pluses and minuses of this type of car, and ask for him to be honest with you in confidence.

Engine repairs are expected, even on a very nice unrestored car. That's how the car survived to the present. Car collectors can accept a modest degree of engine work, such as ground valves, a ring job, maybe even re-sleeved cylinders, plus rebuilt starter, generator and carburetor. None of this will change the car's unrestored condition in the minds of most collectors. That is, as long as replacement components were stock for the era.

Also, examine the appearance of electrical wiring. Is it the type used by the car company in that era? If some re-wiring is needed, can the wire type be matched?

Owning an unrestored car brings special privileges in preservation. What owners discover is that they are caretakers of a piece of history, perhaps even better for reference than an ancient car manual or repair book. They tend to a piece of lively motoring history, cruising the streets and roads of America much as it did ages ago, when life seemed simpler and much more predictable.

A warning list for old rubber

■ There are some car collectors who still prefer to use their car's original radiator hoses, even if they are more than a half-century old. Those were seldom high-pressure cooling systems, and owners who drive their "originals" around town on occasion may get away with the old hoses for long years. But don't press your luck on a long trip in the summer when consistently high operating temperatures may finally split a hose.

■ Similar caution needs to be used with original tires still pounding the road. If a 40-year-old original car has its first set of tires, those may be hard, less prone to gripping the pavement in a panic stop, and could be developing structural cracks that are difficult to notice. Old tires bear careful watching and, when necessary, replacement. Safety is of prime concern. If the old tires are still cosmetically nice, have them demounted and keep them as long as you like. Should you sell your old car, the next owner may like the option of obtaining those original tires for display purposes.

■ Unrestored cars from the 1950s and earlier used real rubber for gaskets and seals around windows, doors, bumper braces, hood corners and other areas. Old rubber loses life, shrinks, dries and contorts over time. Hence, if you plan to drive your car

Getting original paperwork, like this owners manual and dealer information, included in a sale is a bonus.

in all sorts of weather, replacement rubber may be a necessity.

■ If you car's old rubber is in wonderful condition but still a bit hard, explore the option of applying preservatives and conditioners to liven the rubber. This may help the rubber swell slightly for a better fit, or may protect the rubber for more years of use against ultra-violet rays and the attacks of time.

■ A telltale sign of rubber deterioration around doors are globs of melted rubber that speckle the running board or door sill.

Unsightly but not hard to clean, this residue means your closed doors may spring leaks in moderate to heavy rainfall. This can irreversibly stain precious original interior door panels. Consider the condition of your car and order replacement rubber as needed. Match the original style when possible.

■ Companies dealing with rubber replacement products or preservatives to protect existing rubber usually advertise in hobby publications such as *Old Cars Weekly*.

Story and photos by Angelo Van Bogart

A DUESENBERG DREAM

After dreaming about owning a Duesenberg, Shawn Miller bought this largely original 1922 Model A with Fleetwood coupe coachwork.

Shawn Miller began collecting cars as a wheel-crazed teenager. His first car was a Standard Avon saloon, bought at the age of 13 with paper route money. He still has that car, and has since added others, but he never thought he'd join the small group of Duesenberg owners.

The Duesenberg purchase took more than paper route money, but his excitement over the car made the wait worthwhile. It was also a bit of a reunion, because Duesenbergs are a part of the Miller family tradition.

"[Duesenbergs] are a legend in our family," Miller said. "My great uncle Fred owned a Duesenberg sometime in the 1940s or '50s, but I have never been able to find a picture of that car."

The Duesenberg now in the Miller family is a 1922 Model A with a Fleetwood rumble seat coupe body. With less than 100 Model A's in existence, early Duesenberg passenger cars are a rarity, even more so than their Model J brethren. Add to that the fact that Miller's car is the only known

Duesenberg passenger cars feature coachwork from other companies, although some of those bodies were pictured in the company's catalog. This coupe features Fleetwood coachwork, and is the only known Duesenberg to carry this style of coachwork from this maker. Fleetwood built several bodies for the Model A chassis, but most of them were open cars, such as roadsters and touring cars, or sedans.

Fleetwood coupe body to exist on a Duesenberg chassis and, for all historians know, it's the only one ever built.

Miller is a lifelong Indianapolis resident, and so it wasn't just the Fleetwood coupe's rarity that attracted him to the car, but also its history.

"I always liked Indiana-built cars, and obviously the Duesenberg would be the ultimate Indiana-built car," Miller said. And when he saw this particular unrestored Duesenberg in 2001, it made a big impression on him.

"I had first spied this beauty three years ago at Hickory Corners when CCCA member Jim Kaufmann of Atlanta let me ride in the rumble seat on a shake-down cruise," Miller said. "As soon as I saw the car, I was intrigued by it.

"Jim is a pretty spirited driver, and after several laps around the track, I asked to be let out. This was the first time I had ridden in a rumble seat, and my first ride in a Duesenberg. I was making plans how to get out of it if it rolled.

"I had expected the car to be pretty prim-

Cast-aluminum hardware lift rumble seat passengers into their perch. Also note the cast gas cap.

itive, and was amazed at its speed and agility," Miller said. "It has an advanced chassis for its time. This car handles really well."

That drive left enough of an impression on Miller that, when he learned of the car's availability, he told Kaufmann he wanted his next ride to be in the driver's seat.

Miller spent the next three years saving up Kaufmann's asking price, but he almost missed the car. By the time Miller had saved enough money to purchase the Duesenberg in 2004, he learned Kaufmann had just sold the car to a dealer. Luckily, a quick call between the dealer and Kaufmann helped move the car to Miller's garage.

Miller's timing got even better. The sale was made right before the Auburn Cord Duesenberg Club Annual Reunion in Auburn, Ind., so he immediately brought the car to the meet where he learned a lot about its history.

"I took it to Auburn as soon as I got it," Miller said, adding that he didn't even take it off the trailer after retrieving it from St. Louis. He headed straight for the ACD Club meet in Auburn.

After unloading the car in Auburn, Miller found out the Duesenberg's battery was dead. Roger Eddy of the Hotel Auburn helped out with a quick battery recharge. Miller then discovered the vacuum fuel pump was empty. With the fuel and battery squared away, Miller was finally ready to have the car certified by the ACD Club. And

A Duesenberg buyer bought the chassis and could demand any kind of coachwork he or she wanted, but the chassis choices were far more limited. In 1922, only Rudge-Whitworth wire wheels were offered, and they're still present on this Model A coupe. Also note the early version of the Duesenberg's trademark "STOP" taillamp.

even though he hadn't purchased the car early enough to register it, the club allowed him to display it in the exhibition category and drive it in the Parade of Classics.

"Bringing the car to Auburn was one of the smartest things I could have done," Miller said. "Auburn is a special place where they'll let you take a car and help you out."

While at the ACD Club meet, Miller learned the car was purchased new, or at least early in its life, by a Mr. McGarvey of Pennsylvania, who owned the car until his death in the 1970s. Bill Harrah purchased the car from McGarvey's estate for Harrah's Sparks, Nev., car collection, and from there, it went to Mark Smith. The car was then sold to a German car collector, who toured through Europe with it. After adding some miles to the odometer, the German owner sold the car back to Smith, who sold the car to Jim Kaufmann of Atlanta. Kaufmann then sold it to Miller.

It was in Europe that the largely original emerald green-and-black Duesenberg received most of the changes it has undergone.

"The seat leather and the top vinyl [are the car's biggest changes]," said Miller. "I guess the car was used to tour and was out in the rain, so it became necessary to re-

The intimate interior has room for two passengers inside, and two in the rumble seat. There are also pull-down curtains at the rear and at each door for the original owner's unknown, but suspicious, intentions.

"It's really an honor to have such a fine example [of an original car]. "

place the top.

"The guy who sold it [to the European owner] said he was sorry he sold it to him, because those parts were fine and shouldn't have needed replacement."

The Fleetwood coupe-bodied Model A also made an impression on another person, who told Miller he remembered seeing the car approximately 40 years ago. His story helped Miller fill in another detail regarding the Model A's wonderful state of preservation.

"A helpful gentleman said he remembered my car from Hershey in the 1960s," Miller said. "He said the owner was evidently feverishly cleaning the car with a disgusted attitude [at the event]. When the gentleman talked to the car's owner, he said [the Duesenberg] had been left outside overnight only twice in its life and, 'I should have known better than to bring it here' [in the rain]."

The care from that long-term owner helps explains why the original green paint on the aluminum body remains in such good condition, as does the paint on the black fenders. Of course, 80-plus years of driving has chipped the green in a few places, but those few spots offer some insight into how the Fleetwood, Pa., coachbuilder created the body.

"Fleetwood was on the edge of paint technology," said Miller. In those spots where the green paint is chipped, a yellow primer can be seen on the body. It's here that Miller notes Fleetwood's advanced paint and primer technology. Obviously, Fleetwood was on to something, because the emerald green paint still shines.

The Duesenberg's paint didn't shine that well when Miller bought the car in 2003. He spent a generous amount of time polishing the car's paint and German silver-plated hardware before the car's first Auburn appearance in almost 50 years to remove oxidation on the car's surface.

"I believe a car deserves to look shiny," Miller said. "It's really an honor to have such a fine example [of an original car]. There's a difference between a ratty original and a fine original car, and I am not the kind of guy who would own a ratty car and not restore it. I think cars should look as they left the factory, and not be left in a decrepit state. I am honored to have a fine original car that shouldn't be messed with."

In addition to cleaning the Duesenberg, Miller plans to continue enjoying the car the way it was meant to be enjoyed — he plans to keep driving it.

"It's a monster. It's a big car, and it's powerful," he said. "So, yes, I do enjoy driving it."

The Duesenberg brothers' race-inspired chassis is paired with overhead-cam, 260-cid straight-eight cranking out 88 hp.

"I never thought I would be able to get a Duesenberg, but I was lucky to get a nice one."

"As far as Model A's go, it's a fairly sporty car," Miller said.

As the proprietor of SignificantCars.com, a business that sells collector cars, Miller said some people were skeptical of his intentions with the Duesenberg.

"When I bought the car, nobody knew if I was going to sell it again or keep it," Miller said. "I sell other people's cars so that I can keep my own. I have somewhere between not enough cars and too many cars, and most of them are what I call 'over-my-dead-body cars.' This is one of them.

"I never thought I would be able to get a Duesenberg, but I was lucky to get a nice one."

Story and photos by Angelo Van Bogart

RHAPSODY IN BLUES

Six Murphy town cars are believed to have been built for the Duesenberg Model J chassis, and this 37,000-mile car is likely the finest remaining example in unrestored condition.

Even without coachwork, the Duesenberg chassis is an orchestra for the eyes. The fenders form visual crescendos at the peaks and decrescendos at their terminating points, all the while harmonizing with the headlight-and-grille ensemble. The climax of its chassis design comes with the staccato hood louvers, which cloak the car's *pièce de résistance*, its apple-green straight-eight engine.

When it came time to clothe the Due-senberg chassis with coachwork, no other company's bodies struck a chord with as many customers as those from Walter M. Murphy. With more than 140 bodies built on the Model J chassis, nobody fit more of its bodies to the Duesenberg chassis than the Pasadena, Calif., coachbuilder.

Anyone with an appreciation for both automobiles and music would certainly have noticed the beauty of a Murphy town car body on the Duesenberg chassis, and

Thanks to the car's original interior, it's easy to collapse into the seats and hear "Rhapsody in Blue" in your head — but only when the Duesenberg's straight-eight isn't running!

one such person did — band leader Paul Whiteman, aka "The King of Jazz."

Whiteman earned his fame and fortune in the "Roaring Twenties." The musician assured himself stardom in 1920 when he sold 2 million copies of his first record, "Whispering — The Japanese Sandman." Then, he guaranteed himself a place in musical history when he commissioned George Gershwin's "Rhapsody in Blue" in 1924. "Rhapsody in Blue" became a hit, and Whiteman's band, The Paul Whiteman Orchestra, used the song as its signature piece.

Other talent, including Bing Crosby, crossed Whiteman's wake, but more notable to car collectors was "Uncle" Tom McCahill, the witty *Mechanix Illustrated* road tester who befriended Whiteman.

Long before he met McCahill, Whiteman had a taste for fine cars. In 1930, Whiteman had a one-of-a-kind Cord L-29 with a Zapon fabric Weymann coupe body in his garage. The Cord was followed by yet another exotic from the Classic era — a Duesenberg.

On July 18, 1933, Whiteman took delivery of a Murphy town car on the long wheelbase. To remind people why he could afford the prosaic Duesenberg, it was painted three shades of blue, while a fourth blue hue covered the chauffeur's seat.

The Murphy town car has never been restored, and its original 420-cid twin-overhead cam straight-eight has propelled the car only 37,000 miles in its lifetime. The engine was advertised as being good for 265 hp.

Unlike some Duesenbergs buyers, Whiteman did not custom order his town car. Serial No. 2469's engine, J-427, was built Oct. 2, 1930, and its body was finished April 22, 1931, at a cost of $3,500 "in the white," a phrase that reflects the car had not been upholstered or painted by the coachbuilder upon its delivery to Duesenberg. The factory installed the body, and the car was inventoried at Duesenberg's New York branch until it was sold to Whiteman approximately two years later. In the interim, the car appeared in at least one factory photograph depicting a woman and a young girl watching their luggage being handled by a bellman while a seated chauffeur looked on.

Whiteman put very few miles on the Duesenberg before it was stored in a Chrysler garage in New York City around 1938. The car's next recorded owner was William Stoop Jr. of Connecticut, who purchased the car in 1959.

Around five years later, Classic car collector Tony Pascucci, also of Connecticut, purchased the car with 24,700 miles on the odometer. It was while the car was in Pascucci's care that a young Richie Clyne spotted the car in all of its beautiful, unrestored

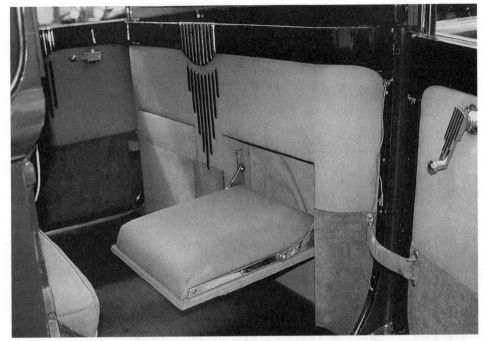

Paul Whiteman was friends with many characters in his lifetime, especially during the 1930s. How many of those important figures rode in the town car's back seat is unknown. But, oh, if the jump seats could talk!

glory. "I had known the car since I was a kid," Clyne said. "Pascucci collected a lot of Isottas and had 10 Duesenbergs. At the time, he had more Duesenbergs than anyone."

But it was the beautifully kept, four-blue Murphy town car that caught Clyne's eye, and when the car became available in 1984, Clyne purchased it for Ralph Englestadt's Auto Collection, which was housed at the Imperial Palace casino. When Englestadt was thinning his collection, Clyne purchased the Duesenberg for himself.

Since the car had been driven very little in more than 50 years, Clyne set out to make

it roadworthy again. Randy Ema, present owner of Duesenberg, installed a new wiring harness, and Brian Joseph installed a high-speed rear end and further serviced the car.

The town car has since been driven in tours all over the world, sometimes in inclement weather, but not completely without trouble.

"Buck Kamphuasen and I have driven it from California to Key West in snow storms," Clyne said.

On one cross-country tour, the town car's rear axle snapped off in a small Kentucky town, but the mishap didn't stop the duo

While the tri-blue exterior serves as an ode to "Rhapsody in Blue," the handsome interior hardware is a reflection of the 1930s art deco movement.

from continuing on the tour.

They found a hotel and rented two rooms — one for themselves, and one for the car.

"We found a hotel and I noticed I could take the doors off and pull the car in [the hotel room]." With the car stored safely, it was time to start tracking down parts.

"I always carry a CCCA directory, and I called Jack Miller and asked if he had any [spare] parts," Clyne said. "Miller didn't have any extra Duesenberg parts, so I figured the best I could do was get an axle from the [Imperial Palace collection]."

In the meantime, Miller took his own Duesenberg apart with his son and freed the car of its axle. The pair left a wedding early and delivered the axle part to Clyne and Kamphausen in their hotel! The group

Former New York City Mayor Jimmy Walker, band leader Paul Whiteman and actress Dolores Del Rio all owned Murphy-bodied Duesenberg town cars like the one in this factory photo.

installed the axle and made it to the starting point of the Millenium Tour in time to complete the tour.

Today, the town car sports around 37,000 miles and remains in excellent, unrestored condition. Like medals on a general's chest, the car proudly wears chips in its blue paint, and wear in the spot where the chauffeur rested his arm.

In his years of being associated with the Auto Collections at the Imperial Palace, Clyne has seen more than 50 Duesenbergs go through its doors.

"Of all the Duesenbergs [in the Auto Collections], it's the only car I remember the J-number of," Clyne said.

Clyne's personal car collection contains several impressive, beautifully restored cars. But if there ever came a time to thin the collection, "The town car will be the last vehicle to leave," Clyne said.

The author would like to extend special thanks to Randy Ema for providing historical information on this Duesenberg.

Story and photos by Peter Winnewisser

YOU'RE NEVER TOO YOUNG FOR A '34 FORD

The 1934 Ford Cabriolet — this one owned by Jason Tagliaferri of Gloversville, N.Y. — is arguably the best looking of the 1934 V-8 passenger cars. Tagliaferri's unrestored car has dual horns, dual cowl lights, dual bumper guards and the V-8 emblem.

The 1934 Fords celebrate their 75th anniversary this year. According to the Ford Motor Co. World Production Report, 563,921 Ford passenger cars rolled off the assembly lines that year. Thousands of them are still in the hands of collectors today, but few are as authentic, even to the original paint in showroom condition, as the 1934 Cabriolet (model 40, type 760) owned by 33-year-old Jason Tagliaferri of Gloversville, N.Y.

Tagliaferri is both a perceptive and patient young man. Perceptive, because he can appreciate the charisma and historical significance of an authentic and original Ford, even though he is, at heart, a street

rod man with a particular love for the Deuce and his 1950 Mercury. Patient, because he spent 10 years of watchful waiting before he was able to make the Cabriolet his own. Here's the story.

The car was assembled in early May of 1934, one of 14,496 produced that year. The factory price was $590. It was sold by Maylender-Hughes dealership in Gloversville, N.Y., to the first owner in late 1934 and then sold two or three months later, in early 1935, to Henry Born Sr.

Born drove the car to church and work. He washed and waxed it every Sunday after church. According to the service records, the car was rarely driven in the winter months.

In the early 1940s it was stored in a garage with about 72,000 miles on the odometer.

The Cabriolet rested in the garage until the mid '80s, when Henry Born Jr., who inherited the car after his father's passing, took it out of storage, rebuilt the engine and brakes and installed a new convertible top and five new tires. He then drove the car sparingly, putting about 2,400 miles on it over 20-plus years.

Tagliaferri and Born met because they stored their cars in the same building. They became friends and kept in touch over a 10-year period during which Tagliaferri, who greatly admired the '34, from time to time expressed his interest in buying the car. In

"I enjoy it very much, it is a piece of history."

October 2007, that hope became a reality.

Since buying the Ford, Tagliaferri has driven it more than 2,000 miles. "I enjoy it very much, it is a piece of history," he said. Last fall, he entered it in the Historic Preservation of Original Features category at the AACA meet in Hershey and won an award. He has the license plates that were on the car when it was sold by the dealer, numerous service records of work done on the car in the early years, the original owner's manual and the installation instructions for the aftermarket Philco radio in the car. In the future, he hopes to replace the new top with the original one, which was taken off only because of a leak. He also has the original boot for the top.

One of the prime features of the car that immediately captures attention is the mostly original Vineyard Green body and wheel color. The paint is spectacular. Possibly, the frequent waxing in the early years helped to preserve it. Except for some paint work on the left front fender in the late 1930s or early '40s due to a minor accident, and the paint on the spare tire cover, the paint is as it

came from the factory. The striping, including the stripes on the hood louvers, is also from the factory.

The upholstery is the original leather and leatherette installed at the factory in both the interior and the rumble seat. The floor mats are also original and in decent condition. The dash has been repainted. The chrome is original. The car currently rides on whitewall tires, but they will eventually be switched to blackwalls. The V-8 power-plant was installed at the factory. It does have 1936 water pumps and the incorrect fuel pump. These will be returned to the factory-installed units, which are in the owner's possession.

Typical of the DeLuxe cars, the Cabriolet has dual horns, cowl lamps, tail lamps, and a chrome-plated windshield frame. The interior has an adjustable seat, cigar lighter, ash tray and glove box. The operating handle for the rumble seat is located behind the passenger side of the front seat. In addition to the radio, accessories include the metal spare tire cover, spare tire lock, bumper guards and the original greyhound grille ornament.

Tagliaferri operates Tag's Upholstery in Gloversville, N.Y., specializing in custom auto, home and boat upholstery. He has restored several cars, including a 1966 Mustang with custom upholstery for his mother. He also helped his father restore a 1957 Ford

"I decided a long time ago that I would never sell the Merc."

retractable, which has won several national awards, including Junior and Senior Awards at AACA meets. About 10 years ago, he built a 1932 Ford three-window coupe from scratch for his brother. Currently, he is working on a 1932 Ford five-window coupe for himself. It will have a stock-looking body, a 302 Ford engine, automatic overdrive and four-wheel independent suspension.

Tagliaferri's first love, however, is his 1950 Mercury, which he has owned since he was 14. "I learned how to weld as I chopped the top on the car when I was 16," he says. "It is now a full custom. I decided a long time ago that I would never sell the Merc, because I've talked to a lot of guys my dad's age or older and they all say the same thing: 'I wish I still had my first car, I never should have sold it.' The Merc is my first car, and I

hope I will be able to continue to say that I own it for a long time."

So there you have the story. A young man who is especially fond of his custom Merc and '32 Ford street rod. He is just 33 years old, with a world of old car experience. He specializes in upholstery work and also has an appreciation for the historical charm of his pristine '34 Ford Cabriolet. It's not just the older generation that has a love for vintage iron.

Note: The author is indebted to the following for background information: Standard Catalog of Ford, 4th edition *by John Gunnell;* The Early Ford V-8 *by Edward Francis and George DeAngelis;* The V-8 Affair *by Ray Miller;* the Ford Motor Company World Production Report, 1903-1955.

Story and photos by Angelo Van Bogart

ONE FOR THE ROAD

The pavement calls out to this 1937 Packard Twelve

**In 70-plus years, this 1937 Packard Twelve Series 1508 Seven Passenger Touring Sedan
traveled less than 38,000 miles. The first 20,000 miles were put on by a funeral home.
All that keeps the car from being completely unrestored is a repaint in the original black
color, applied one year before its current owners purchased the car in 1973,
and a recent engine rebuild.**

F̲ew collectors can crack open their garage and look at the elegant radiators of restored V-12 Cadillac roadsters, big 1934 Packards, a supercharged Cord, Auburn speedster and even a Duesenberg convertible sedan all at once. Dave and Marlese Lindsay of Manawa, Wis., are among those fortunate but rare collectors.

But with all of this heavy iron, it's not the colorful speedster or the V-16 Cadillac All-Weather Phaeton or the two-tone rose-colored Model J Duesenberg that the Lindsays pick to drive when the two-lane roads around their home call — it's the jet-black, largely original 1937 Packard Twelve Series 1508 Seven Passenger Touring Sedan they fancy.

"When somebody says, 'Bring an old car,' it's the car we drive," Dave said. "It's dependable, reliable, comfortable and it has a heater. And, basically, everything works."

And drive it he does. Since buying the formal Packard in October 1973 with around 20,000 miles on the odometer, he's logged an additional 17,000 miles in tours, travels to car shows and Sunday drives.

When the car was photographed for this story, it had just returned from a 900-plus-mile Classic Car Club of America "See the USA the Hoosier Way CARavan" around Indiana. The 2007 event marked the second time the Packard Twelve has logged around 1,000 miles in a tour since Lindsay bought it more than three decades ago.

As it always does, the Packard and its 473-cid, 175-hp 12-cylinder engine performed flawlessly on the journey. Lindsay said the engine was rebuilt several years ago, and during its tour around Indiana, it only consumed about one quart of oil. A

This Packard carries a Body No. 1034. It was delivered late in the 1937 model year, according to its data plate on the cowl, which lists a delivery date of November 3 and a delivery location of Oshkosh, Wis.

This Packard seven-passenger sedan carries a touring steering wheel, while more sporting Packards from 1937 were equipped with banjo-style steering wheels. All of the lights and gauges on the symmetrically pleasing instrument panel remain in fine working order, though they have never been opened up for repair. Even the radio still sings. The gauge faces match the shape of the steering wheel hub, which matches the gear shift knob.

perfect quantity, in Lindsay's estimation.

"Packard wanted these engines to use one quart of oil every 1,000 miles or so, and that's how they knew they were properly lubricated," he said.

It's very likely that the Twelve's first owner never drove it more than 100 miles at a time, let alone 1,000 miles. The Lindsays purchased the car from its original owner, the Spikes & McDonald Funeral Home in Oshkosh, Wis., which used the stately Packard Twelve to carry mourners and pall-bearers.

The comforting touches included inside

this noble Packard for funeral processions are evident throughout. There are shades for the rear-most side windows and back window, jump seats to accommodate up to seven passengers, rich walnut trim and even small, round mirrors for passengers to powder their noses before stepping out of the car. These mirrors fit perfectly into slots in the rear armrests, which also hold an ash receiver and cigar lighter on each side. Like the rest of the interior, all of these details are in marvelous, original condition and remain just as Packard employees installed

This car's original interior has been referenced by restorers working to authentically reupholster concours-winning cars. The art deco accelerator pedal appears to borrow its design from the Chrysler Building.

them 70 years ago.

Given its intended purpose, it's not surprising that the car has been so well preserved. Often, cars used by funeral homes are maintained to a very high standard, and this Packard was no different. What does surprise Lindsay is that the car is equipped with a high-speed rear end, which makes the car's modern purpose of touring more enjoyable. Unfortunately, he wasn't able to learn why the car was equipped with the highway-friendly rear end.

"By the time I became interested in learning the car's history, a couple years after I bought it, the funeral home had been sold," Lindsay said. He also never had the chance to meet the

Packard was very good at coordinating the car's components. The material used to line the trunk matches the materials used in the passenger compartment, both of which are the factory-installed materials on this car. The tool bag on the floor holds the original jack components.

original owners, as the car was advertised in *Old Cars Weekly* by a third party, who was storing the Packard for the funeral home.

Other aspects of the Packard make it a joy for touring. Their Packard Twelve's chassis includes the new-for-'37 Safe-T-FleX independent front suspension, which offered a smoother ride than models from the previous year.

"Those changes make all the difference in the world," Lindsay said. "When you go over railroad tracks with this car, you can barely feel them under the car, not like a modern car." The old sedan can keep up with those modern cars, too.

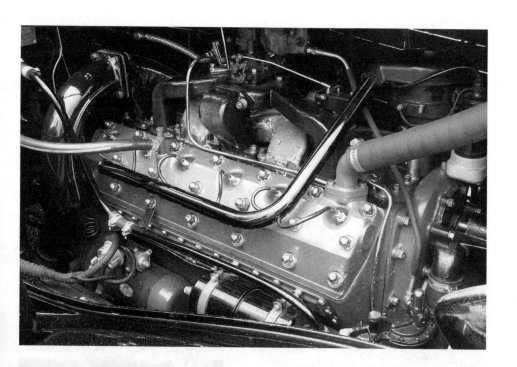

"This thing has more 'oomph' [than my 1934 Packard Twelve convertible coupe]," he said.

I can attest to that. Lindsay offered me a seat behind the comfortable wheel of his 1937 Packard. After sliding the car into high gear, I pushed down on the art-deco aluminum accelerator pedal, and the 6,500-pound Packard responded like a whipped horse, though in a much more smooth and quiet manner.

"If you're idling along, you can get within 5 feet of people before they hear you coming," Lindsay said.

When those people do sense the Packard, they stop, pause and admire the stately car and all of its presence, giving this handsome car the appreciation it has earned.

Story and photos by John Gannell

ONE-IN-A MILLION ORIGINAL

'38 Buick Special business coupe

This low-mileage, original 1938 Buick carries a grille that is heavier-looking than those on 1937 models.

"**I** just wanted a car that was nice and original," says John Merrick of Fremont, Wis. "But even I couldn't believe there was something as nice as this 1938 Buick Special business coupe — until I saw it in person." According to Merrick, the dark-green five-window coupe exceeded his every expectation.

The 62,000-original-mile car is not the first '38 Buick Merrick owned. "I had a nicely restored 1938 four-door convertible that John Koutrie had owned," he says, referring to a well-known Wisconsin car collector. "That car started with almost no floor and received a great restoration. But it never ran the way the coupe does, which shows one of the advantages of an original car."

The coupe was purchased from a man in Minnesota, but it came from California in 1994, and Merrick still has the California title. "It was always kept out there until the point it was sold to the Minnesota man," he notes. "He was a bachelor who took great care of everything he owned, including his motor home. He also had a real nice '34 Buick and an extremely nice '35 Buick four-door sedan with 43,000 original miles."

The '38 Buick is very original, down to its paint and factory pinstriping. The body finish shines like only the old Duco nitro-cellulose lacquer can, but there is crazing and "hen's feet" cracks in areas around the factory-leaded body seams and on the curved surface below the rear window on the driver's side.

Older California plates on the rear go well with the Buick's high degree of originality.

The car's upholstery, headliner and wood-grain dashboard
finish have all been preserved in very nice condition.

"I just wanted a car that was nice and original. But even I couldn't believe there was something as nice as this 1938 Buick Special business coupe — until I saw it in person."

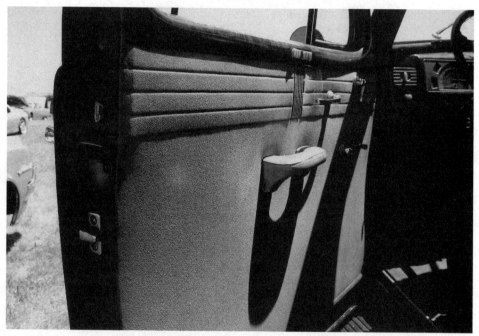

They're only original once, and one of the beauties of finding a well-preserved car is that all of the trim details look factory correct.

Merrick has owned the car for two years. "I changed the oil, cleaned it and drove it," he says. "The seller had already gone through the fan belts and cooling system hoses. The man who had it in California put $1,500 into the brakes back in 1992, so they are great." Merrick — who deals in wood boats and collector cars — says the car stays in a big, locked garage all year.

The Special two-door business coupe, Model 38-46, has front Ventipanes, lowerable door glass, small rear quarter windows and a spare tire in the trunk.

Merrick's car is one of 11,337 made. This model retailed for $945 and had a shipping weight of 3,385 lbs. All 1938 Buicks were distinguished by a new two-piece die-cast grille with wider horizontal grille bars

The original GM nitrocellulose lacquer tends to "alligator" in spots where the factory used lead under the paint to fill in body seams, such as below the rear windows.

spaced farther apart. Longer bullet-shaped headlamps were mounted integral with the radiator shell.

Technical advances for 1938 included a full coil-spring suspension. An Automatic Safety Transmission was offered for Specials, although most people preferred the standard three-speed manual. All models had all-steel Unisteel body construction and Fisher Body Turret Top styling. Batteries were moved from beneath the floorboards to under the hood, and all Buicks had hypoid rear axles.

The Special engine was a 248-cid valve-in-head inline eight with a 6.15:1 compres-

sion ratio and a Marvel CDI or Stromberg AAV-1 dual-downdraft carburetor. It produced 107 hp at 3,400 rpm and 203 lbs.-ft. of torque at 2,000 rpm.

In addition to his 1938 Buick Special coupe, Merrick owns a 1955 Cadillac, a pair of 1961 Corvettes, a 1967 Corvette and a 1971 Corvette. He says he's looking for another 1938 Buick four-door convertible that's "real nice and original."

That's his dream car, but his coupe is a reality that he's very happy with. "They're only original once," he reminds us. "And this is a nice one, especially for a business coupe."

Stories and photos by Angelo Van Bogart

HAVING A GAS IN A BONE-STOCK WILLYS

Nathan Van Bogart photo

After more than 65 years, this Willys retains nearly all of its original paint. Its current owner, Al Lindgren, owns a second Willys coupe that was a gasser in the 1960s. That car is being revived to gasser configuration, but the coupe pictured here will remain stock as long as it's in Lindgren's hands. Lindgren tracked this car's history back to the original owner, a Willys dealer who sold only two cars, including this one.

In a sea of shiny pro-street and gasser-style Willyses painted bright reds and yellows, Al Lindgren's unrestored, ghostly Bedford Gray 1941 Willys Americar coupe, with all of its chips and dings and its skinny bias-ply tires, is the star of the show.

And unlike those other Willys owners, Lindgren didn't have to re-engineer his Willys' suspension, cut its body to fit bigger meats or build an early Hemi engine for the coupe to attract a crowd. He barely had to track down any parts, let alone paint

It's hard to believe now, but the 1937 and 1938 Willyses, which shared basic body shells with this 1941 Americar, were voted as the worst-looking cars those years in an annual poll taken at the New York Auto Show by the Market Research Corp. There's no question that the Willys' design has proven timeless, and that revised front sheet metal in 1940 only made what many now consider to be a good thing even better. This particular '41 Willys is so original, it still retains its optional exhaust tailpipe extension.

the coupe. In fact, the less he does to it, the more it stands out.

To find out how Lindgren's Willys coupe remained one of the finest original '41 Willys coupes, one need only to trace its tracks from the start. Luckily, Lindgren has done that.

In the early 1940s, Chris Nelson from Canton, S.D., received a license to distribute Willys vehicles. According to Lindgren's research, the penny-wise Nelson wanted the license only to get a better deal on a new car. Willys required its licensees to purchase at least two vehicles, so Nelson bought two coupes, the most affordable body style from America's least-expensive full-size marque.

As required, two Willyses arrived at Nelson's South Dakota business from Willys' Toledo assembly line: a blue coupe and the gray coupe pictured here. Nelson kept the blue coupe for himself, and it was eventually destroyed in a garage fire during the 1950s. The gray coupe was sold to Nelson's brother Herman, who kept the miles low.

The upholstery and much of the interior remains as original as the outside. By the owner's count, the car is on its third set of seat covers over the original seat material. The door pull straps were a $1.75 option. The trunk is cavernous, but is it large enough to sleep in? The second owner's family thought so and camped out here on occasion. Under the original tools and reproduction trunk mat, the car's current owner found previous owners' names scratched into the paint. The names are still there.

From 1941-'59, Herman only put 21,000 miles on the Willys, and from 1959-'67, he added only 800 more to the odometer. All the while, Herman kept the car serviced and in a heated garage.

By the late 1960s, Herman had probably endured countless offers from drag racers to buy his Willys coupe, but he re-

The seal between the door vent glass and side glass is incorporated into the side window for a clean and sporty look with the windows down.

sisted every one of them. Since the 1950s, the type of people who would give a Willys a second look were drag racers with thoughts of Hemi engines and Oldsmobile rear ends dancing in their heads. Thanks to the Willys' featherweight status and short wheelbase length, which actually aided traction at drag strip Christmas trees, Willyses were the perfect drag cars, never mind the fact that they looked good doing it.

It took more than a stock engine to move the Willys, however. The 63-hp four-cylinder installed by the factory into every 1941 Willys was good for puttering along back roads at a decent clip, but as the number of freeways (and their speed limits) increased, driving an old and stock Willys may have seemed like a liability more than a leisure activity. From this line of thinking, many drag racers probably felt they were performing a service by modifying Willyses.

When Herman Nelson finally did sell his Willys in 1967, it wasn't to a drag racer or street rodder — it was to Sonny Hagseth, his great nephew. Herman cut Sonny a sweet deal on the 21,700-mile Willys and handed over the car and title for only $200.

The car's age and low sale price didn't prevent Sonny from trusting its dependability. He used the car on several trips, and he

"As that garage door opened, I can only imagine what was going through Dexter's mind at the time. There sat an original, stock, all-steel, uncut [Willys]."

and his family often slept in the car's cavernous trunk on overnight trips. Lindgren learned from Sonny that the car would happily cruise at 60 mph.

By this time, Willyses were becoming well known as good drag machines, and Sonny must have been tempted to check out the drag racing experience for himself. In 1968, he took the still-stock car to the Thunder Valley Drag Strip and entered it in U/Stock, where he was pitted against a VW Beetle. While the Willys made an impressive show of spinning one of its rear tires, it lost the race to the Beetle. Luckily, that was the end of this Willys' gasser experience.

In 1972, Sonny decided to start a construction business, so he placed a "for sale" sign in the Willys' window. In Sioux Falls, the car caught the attention of Joe Castle, a service station owner. Castle bought the car for $1,500 and scratched his name in the trunk before selling it four years later. Thanks to his mark, Lindgren was able to trace each of the car's owners and nearly all of its blemishes, right down to a ding on the front fender.

Word of Castle's ownership of the Willys spread as far as California, and around 1976, he received a call from Ted Shafer, a jazz musician in San Francisco's Ted Shafer's Jelly Roll Jazz Band, asking if Castle would sell the car. Shafer already owned a 1941 Willys sedan and wanted to add a coupe to his collection, but was having a difficult time finding a stock Willys coupe in California. After Castle agreed to put new tires on the car and fix a dent in the trunk lid (the car's only known paint work), a deal was struck, and Shafer flew up to South Dakota intending to drive the Willys back. He got as far as the border between Utah and Nevada before the engine seized. Apparently, Shafer forgot to check the oil, so after the car was flat-bedded to San Francisco, the engine was rebuilt with the odometer at 36,000 miles.

Shafer sold the car in the latter part of the 1970s, though he can't recall why, and it passed through several other California owners' hands. One of those owners worked at an aquatic park, where the car attracted more than its share of looks in the parking lot. By the 1980s, the Willys was anything but camera shy, having had many lenses pointed at it.

Californian Willys owner Dexter Ben-

The round-cornered razor grille and teardrop-shaped headlamps of the 1941 Willys perfectly harmonize with the car's bow-edged hood. Note the Americar name on the leading edge of the hood.

nett first spotted the unrestored '41 coupe in 1987 from one of the many photographs snapped of the car. Bennett ran across the photograph a second time in 1989 and felt inspired to track it down through its license plate. Police were able to give him a name and address for the owner, so Bennett took this information to a title company to track down the phone number. After making several phone calls and sending many letters to the owner, Bennett bought the car without ever having seen it in person.

"In the spring of 1991, Dexter [Bennett] and two friends set out on the five-hour drive one-way to pick up the car," Lindgren said. "As that garage door opened, I can only imagine what was going through Dexter's mind at the time. There sat an original, stock, all-steel, uncut [Willys]."

In the nine years Bennett owned the Willys, he replated the bumpers, polished the stainless trim and went through the car's mechanic bits with the goal of preservation.

"He even went as far as reproducing dash knobs, the trunk mat and rubber bushings and grommets exactly as original," Lindgren said.

Rumors began to circulate in the late 1990s of Bennett's interest in selling the Willys. Since Lindgren was already resur-

"It's had some stuff redone, but even a 65-year-old man has had a little dental work done, too."

recting a period gasser and was driving a stock 1942 sedan, he was tightly tied into the Willys clubs and acted on the rumors by contacting Bennett.

"[Sellers] don't advertise their Willys for sale much," Lindgren said. "They're sold under the wraps. It's difficult to buy a stock one, and if you mention 'hot rod' to the seller, you're probably not going to get one."

But already owning a stock Willys wasn't enough to sway Bennett into signing the title over to Lindgren, at least right away.

"[The owner] was more eccentric than most of them, but he knew I had an interest in originality," Lindgren said. "I had to actually prove myself and that I was not going to hot rod the [car]."

It took a while for Lindgren and Bennett to get to know each other, but it was time well spent. After several phone calls over an extended period of time, Bennett agreed to sell the Willys to Lindgren.

With the sale price agreed upon, it was only a matter of shipping the Willys from Bennett's California home to Lindgren's Minnesota garage. But there was one hitch — Lindgren hadn't seen the car in person, and Bennett was reluctant to ship it before Lindgren could lay eyes on it.

"I think he thought I thought I was going to get it and think it was going to be a pris-tine show car," Lindgren said. But the Minnesotan knew it was a 60-year-old survivor and was confident the South Dakota and California climates had preserved it well. He was not disappointed, although he grew nervous when the car arrived at his home.

"When the truck pulled up, I started getting a little freaked out, because it was a lot of money for a car I hadn't seen personally," Lindgren admitted. However, several friends Lindgren trusted had seen the car and had walked away impressed. Lindgren had also seen the car in a video.

When the enclosed carrier opened up, Lindgren's nerves got to him. Was the video as thorough as he'd hoped? Were his friends' definitions of a "nice" car the same as his? He was about to find out.

"When it showed up, it was in the middle of the truck with a plastic car cover on it, and I started getting weak in the knees," he said. "But as soon as I could see [how nice] the rear fender down by the door was, I was so happy. It was everything I thought it would be as a survivor."

There were some problems, however. The car's brake pedal went down to the floor, and there were no keys or gas in the tank. It seems Bennett hadn't trusted sending the car with its keys and title, but he perfectly timed the shipping of all the items.

47

The dimensions of the Willys' frame and its body shell were largely unchanged from 1937 to 1942, and because the wheelbase was stretched from 100 inches in 1937 and '38 to 102 inches in 1939 and 104 inches in 1941 and '42, the rear wheels are not centered in the wheel opening on later cars. Although the car's third set of whitewalls have yellowed with time, its owner has been encouraged to leave them on the car to add to its patina.

The keys arrived in the mail just behind the semi loaded with the Willys.

"That night, I looked out the garage door [to see the car] about 50 times all night," Lindgren said.

Once the car was nestled in its new home, Lindgren began to make it a little bit better than when it arrived, but he, too, worked on it with preservation rather than restoration in mind.

"It's had some stuff redone, but even a 65-year-old man has had a little dental work done, too," he said. In the years he's owned the Willys coupe, Lindgren has merely washed and tinkered with it...and driven it!

"I went through the brakes and put a correct radio in it, but I did not put an antenna on it because you have to put holes [in the body]. The hood never fit right, which you can see in old photos, so I had to do a little tweaking to get it to fit like it should," he said.

Lindgren has been attracted to Willyses since he saw a picture of Ohio George Montgomery's '33 Willys coupe model kit as a kid. He even thought to himself, "Some day I'll own one." Yet he freely admits that

"You've got to keep the [Willys] survivors the way they are."

Willyses were economy cars built with frugality in mind.

"These were Kleenex cars — use 'em up and throw 'em away," he said. "They were a cheap car built in a depressed time in Toledo. A lot of people think that hot rodding used up all these cars, and [while] a great majority were rodded, I think hot rodding saved a lot of them. Otherwise, they would have been crushed."

But hot rodding is something that will never happen to this car as long as it's parked in Lindgren's garage.

"You've got to keep the [Willys] survivors the way they are," Lindgren said. "A lot of people would have taken it to a hot rodder and not given it a second thought as to what the history of the car is or where it came from."

Through his connections with Willys collectors, Lindgren estimates there are approximately 15 unrestored and driving 1940-'42 coupes known to Willys zealots. There are probably only a handful more restored Willys coupes, so leaving a car like this untouched helps illustrate the rarely explored history of the marque.

"The rocker panels on my car are completely different from other 1941 Willys rocker panels," he said. "It's a very late serial-numbered car, so it could have been one of the last '41s. The 1941s came standard with rocker panels, and running boards were optional. In '42, running boards were standard, and rocker panels were optional. Coming out of the Depression and going into war times, who knows how these ended up on this car?"

For Lindgren, part of the joy of owning the unrestored Willys comes from the reaction of crowds who see the 54,000-mile coupe when he shows it.

"Every kid looks at it, and everyone [else] who looks at it says, 'I'd like to get a Willys,'" Lindgren said. "For some reason, these things grab a hold of you."

And it's clear this one isn't letting go of Lindgren's affection anytime soon.

Story by Brian Earnest

'DREAM DEALS' REALLY DO HAPPEN

Fred Lossman bought his 1955 Chevrolet Bel Air two-door sedan from a Kansas couple who trusted him with not only the keys to the car, but also the keys to their home and Cadillac. The Chevy has just 19,000 miles on the odometer.

Fred Lossman has one of those stories that is just so hard to believe and "out there," you know that is has to be true. Nobody would believe him if he just made the whole thing up.

It isn't just that Lossman wound up with a splendid, extremely collectible, low-mileage, all-original 1955 Chevrolet Bel Air two-door sedan. That would be amazing enough, regardless of how he got it. But it's how he got it that's so mind-boggling.

His tale is classic example of the trust "car folks" often have in other car folks, even if they've never even met; and the enduring truth that you never know for sure what you'll find when you take a chance

and go look at an old car.

Lossman's part of the story started back in 1998, when the resident of Nevada City, Calif., was checking out some online classified ads and came across a simple two-sentence ad for a 1955 Bel Air. "The ad said something like, '1955 Chevy, 12,000 original miles, stick shift,' and it had a phone number," Lossman recalled. "And that's about all it said."

We'll let Lossman narrate what happened from there.

"In 1955, the car was bought by a woman in Salina Kansas. She did laundry for a living, and was described as a feisty, Irish woman, and she saved her money to buy this car. And after she purchased it, she wouldn't let anybody ride in it, even her husband! In fact, there had never been anybody ever ride in it. She kept the car until 1987, and then she went into a rest home. The couple that I bought the car from [also from Salina] purchased it in 1987. The woman bought it for her husband's 60th birthday, as a surprise for him.

"At that point — this is in 1987 — it had 11,100 miles. So it went from 1955 to 1987 with this woman driving with nobody else in the car, until it had 11,100 miles. Then this couple in Kansas had it, and the guy drove it once a year in a parade. That was it. That was about all they drove it."

And that's about the time Lossman saw the ad saying the car was for sale.

"I'm one of these guys that is just constantly screening car ads," he said. "I've known Chevys all my life, and '55 is kind of known as a premier year. It was just a flyer I called on to see what the deal was ... I called the phone number and it was a guy in San Diego, and he said he was just placing the ad for his uncle. So I called the folks in Kansas and talked to the husband that owned the car. He was somewhat grouchy, because I kept asking about he condition of the car, and he kept saying 'It's only got 12,000 miles!'

"So I used some airline miles and flew to Kansas and they had arranged to meet me at the airport ... We drove to their city and checked into a motel, and the woman picked me up the next morning, and she said. 'I have to go to work, and we'll drive by the bank where I work, I'm going to leave the car with you for the day.' And she gave me the keys to the [Bel Air], her house and her Cadillac! She said, 'Make yourself comfortable!' So, I drove to the house, and looked at the garage and saw the Chevy. It was covered up, but I could see it. I didn't have the nerve to start it without the owners being home, but I was sure tempted. When the man came home from work we took it for a ride. We took it out on the freeway. Obviously, the front end was shot. It was wandering all over the place. But it sounded good, was reasonably clean ... I had no conception as to what I was going to find. I thought it

would be rusty and original, but would need a lot of work. I was amazed at the condition of the car. I played it very cool, because I thought this guy was going to be grouchy, and he was…

"Later, we drove back to the airport and I made an offer. He didn't accept, and he was kind of grouchy, and I thought I screwed up …. When I got home I called the woman back the next day, and told her I wanted to buy the car … The man didn't like people from California because he was sure I was going to turn it into a hot rod …and I was a surfer. So I sent him pictures of my '61 Chevy pickup, which was a national award winner … and gave him a sob story about how I wouldn't turn his car into a hot rod."

Well, the Kansas couple did finally agree to sell their Chevy, and the retired Lossman has turned the Bel Air into a bit of a time capsule. Today, the car has just 19,000 miles, and almost everything that isn't disposable remains original: it's two-tone paint (Neptune Green with Seafoam Green), chrome, engine, running gear and interior.

"I did the ball joints. I had the gas tank boiled. I replaced the gas gauge, because it didn't work. I replaced the hoses and anything rubber on it that needed replacing. I tuned it, and I spent hours polishing the paint," Lossman said. "The interior didn't need anything, but I did put seat belts in it. And it had the original bias tires on it, so I replaced them with radials, so I could drive

it. It had blackwalls, but I put whitewalls on it."

Any of the "Tri-Five' Chevrolets are a hit with enthusiasts today, but two-door sedans like Lossman's were not exactly the glamour cars of the period, nor were they the most popular. Plenty of the two-door post sedans were sold for 1955 (168,313), but both the four-door sedan (345,372 units) and two-door hardtop (185,562) were more popular in Chevy's top-of-the-line Bel Air series. Today, the two-door sedans take a backseat in the collecting world to the hardtops and con-

vertibles of the era, but cars as well preserved as Lossman's '55, are hot tickets.

"I belong to a Chevy club, and some of the guys have cars of that vintage, but most of them are hopped up," Lossman said. "Mine is the rarity of the bunch. Most people would pull that [six-cylinder] engine out and drop a V-8 into it, but I would never do that."

"One of the dilemmas I have is that I like to brag about the low mileage it has, which means I shouldn't drive it," he added with a chuckle. "Pretty soon it is going to turn

"Mine is the rarity of the bunch. Most people would pull that [six-cylinder] engine out and drop a V-8 into it, but I would never do that."

over 20,000 miles… It's pretty silly trying to explain that to my wife."

Lossman's car is powered by Chevy's 123-horsepower, 235.5-cid six-cylinder, and has a three-speed with overdrive and single-barrel carburetor. A three-speed manual gearbox with column-mounted gearshift was standard on all models for 1955. Overdrive was available on the manual transmission at $108 extra. A Powerglide two-speed automatic transmission was available at $178 extra.

The 265-cid V-8 engine was available in 1955 with an optional "power-pack" that included single four-barrel carburetor and dual exhaust.

Standard equipment on the Bel Airs included most features found on the lower-priced lines, plus: carpets on closed body styles; chrome ribbed headliners on the Sport Coupe; richer upholstery fabrics; horizontal chrome strip on the sides of the front fender and doors; narrow white painted inserts on the rear fender horizontal side moldings; gold Bel Air script and a Chevrolet crest behind the slanting vertical sash molding; ribbed vertical trim plate on the sides above the rear bumper ends; wide chrome window and door post reveals and full wheel discs.

"Mine doesn't even have an oil filter because it I think cost an extra 2 dollars and 50 cents when it was new," Lossman joked.

Lossman says his car is not quite perfect, but he has no plans to fix its few small flaws. "There is a scratch on the front bumper and a small dent about the size of the dime on the top of one fender — just a tiny little dimple, like somebody maybe dropped something on it," he said. "Other than that, it looks new … I put a lot of hours into (the paint). I was surprised how well it turned out. I thought I'd take too much off it, because I'm not a professional paint and body guy. But the paint really turned out great. The hood is showing some signs of age. There is some swirl marks, but the rest of it pretty much looks like new."

Amazingly, Lossman has even kept up a bit of a friendship with the former owners, even the "grouch" who was so reluctant to sell him the car in the first place. "I've kept in contact with and send them pictures of them periodically from car shows," he said. "It's kind of a dream deal, really."

Story and photos by Angelo Van Bogart

À LA CARTE DODGE

A 1957 Dodge D-500 convertible ordered for a young man's right foot

Estimates put only five 1957 Dodge D-500 Custom Royal convertibles with the dual-carburetor 325-cid, 310-hp Hemi on the road in 1957. This original car has traveled less than 15,000 miles and seen only two different garages in its lifetime.

Warren A. Harmon knew what he wanted when he bought a new car in 1957. And when he finally got it, he kept it new for nearly 50 years.

After he graduated from the University of Wisconsin at Milwaukee, Harmon's parents told him he could have any car he wanted. It was a dream situation, and Harmon took advantage of the opportunity.

Harmon walked into Edwards Motors and ordered a black 1957 Dodge Custom Royal convertible. Not a new Thunderbird. Not a Chrysler 300-C. Not a fuel-injected Corvette. Instead, he ordered the flashiest version of a working man's Dodge.

"I asked [Harmon] why he didn't get a Corvette, and he said his parents were buying the car for him, and they said he could get any car he wanted, but he loved Lawrence Welk," said Bob Brown, who, along with George Collar, are the second and current owners of the Dodge. "At that time,

The original owner of the Dodge, Warren A. Harmon, is pictured at left with one of the car's present owners, Robert Brown, in 2005. This 1957 photograph, taken by the original owner after he purchased the car, could have been taken yesterday, because the unrestored car hasn't changed. Only the tires are different.

Dodge sponsored Lawrence Welk's TV show, and [Harmon] liked watching Lawrence Welk driving Dodges on TV."

Even though Welk's audience for his "Dodge Dancing Party" show was slightly older than the recent college graduate, Harmon wanted power like every other twenty-something. He just chose to get it from a Dodge, rather than 'Vette or a Chrysler 300.

Harmon selected black paint and red interior on a D-500 convertible. But he stopped checking boxes shortly after the 310-hp multi-carburetor D-500 Hemi engine option.

"I think he basically ordered it power delete," Brown said. "He bought the biggest engine option — it's a Hemi with dual four-barrel carburetion — and eliminated anything that took away power [from the engine]." That meant no air conditioning, no power brakes and no power steering.

What Harmon did next is probably baf-fling to anyone who didn't understand his madness, including the factory: He specified that his Dodge be equipped with a standard transmission.

"Harmon said the automatic transmission took away power, and he wanted it with the max power he could get," Brown said.

Few people would order Dodge's most expensive model, the D-500 Custom Royal convertible, with a manual transmission, so when the car came down the line, Harmon said factory workers fit it with the Torque-Flite transmission instead.

The shiny black 1957 Dodge Custom Royal showed up at Edwards Motors' new car lot with the wrong transmission, however. He refused delivery and made the salesman order the car again. An automatic transmission simply didn't fit his vision of the perfect car.

Harmon and the salesman went back to the order sheet and began checking those

Warren A. Harmon had to order this Dodge twice to get the manual transmission, because the factory didn't believe he intended to order the manual transmission and built an automatic transmission version of the car. That means a TorqueFlite twin to this car was built. Does it still exist?

same precious few boxes. It took around five months for the next black 1957 Dodge D-500 Custom Royal with a red interior to show up on Edwards Motors' lot, but when it did late in the model year, it carried the correct transmission.

"The gave [Harmon] a dealer add-on spotlight with a mirror on the back, because it took so long to get the car," Brown said. As was customary in the 1950s, the dealer also added a plaque to the glove box with Harmon's name on it. And in place of the push-button gear selector, the Dodge wore a matching delete plate, just how Harmon hoped it would.

The wait must have been difficult. Perhaps he stopped in on a regular basis to ask the salesman how his car was coming and if he had heard when it might be delivered. The visits may have started at month intervals, then weeks, and then down to days until the Dodge finally showed up. We'll never know, but Brown does know that Harmon still knew the salesman well enough to have his current phone number on hand almost 50 years after the car was delivered.

With the jet black Dodge finally in his hands, Harmon began piloting his Forward-Look Mopar to his new job. Then disaster struck.

"About the third or fourth week into his new job, he drove it to work and somebody put a scratch in the passenger side," Brown said. "After that, he drove it home

On the trunk lid, and in the shadow of the towering Swept-Wing Dodge tailfins, was the D-500 emblem, denoting the presence of either the 285-hp, single-four-barrel 325-cid Hemi or the 310-hp dual-four-barrel version of the same engine. This unrestored Dodge sports the former. To cover the location of the push-button controls for the TorqueFlite when the three-speed was specified, this plate was devised.

and parked it. Harmon told me he went out and bought a beater and drove that to work from then on."

The scratch, which still remains, isn't that big, but it was enough for Harmon to keep the car out of the rain and in its heated garage. A sticker on the door jam shows the car had registered only 13,000 miles in 1962. Today, it has slightly more than 14,000 spins on the odometer. Brown said many of those miles put on by 1962 were acquired by Harmon driving the car between Milwaukee and Madison to keep it exercised. Since the

additional 1,000 miles were put on between 1962 and 2004, when Brown and Collar purchased the car, Harmon likely admired his Dodge like a knickknack for the last 42 years of his ownership.

Brown and Collar learned of this well-preserved original car through Larry Fissett, who has a strong nose for sniffing out great automotive finds. (Fissett is best known for finding and purchasing 21 trailers of muscle cars and parts in 2005.) Knowing Brown and Collar were into collecting finned Mopars, Fissett called and asked if they would be in-

The bright red original interior has been preserved by seat covers since new.

terested in adding the very special Dodge to their collection. Knowing how difficult it is to find such cars, the partners jumped at the chance.

Fissett acted as the go-between, but Brown stayed on the hard-to-reach Harmon, promising the car would go to a good home. It took nearly as long to close the deal as it did for the Dodge to be delivered to Edwards Motors' car lot back in 1957, but Brown and Collar finally landed their "Swept-Wing Dodge" in 2004.

Once Harmon parted with his Dodge, Fissett took the car into his shop and replaced all the rubber parts that had rotted over time. Belts around the 325-cid V-8's pulleys con-

tracted for the first time since they were new, nearly 50-year-old tires exhaled 1957 air and the engine saw its first change of hoses.

"We replaced everything that had to be replaced to make it mechanically sound," Brown said.

The car is in truly extraordinary condition. When I first spotted the car a few years ago in the Historic Preservation of Original Features class at an Antique Automobile Club of America meet in Rochester, Minn., I was convinced it was a restored car that had been placed in the incorrect class. I was wrong, of course, but given the car's outstanding condition, it's a frequent mistake. Brown and Collar respect the car's original condition, and work diligently to maintain its high level of preservation.

"Unfortunately, we consider it a trailer queen," said Brown. "We only bring it to a couple of shows a year — Iola [Old Car Show] and concourses. I think we've put a whopping 200 miles on it since we've had it.

"People at the Rochester meet of the AACA said it's the kind of car you look at to see what they're supposed to look like."

Factory records do not break down Dodge production by body style within a series, so it's difficult to say how many Dodge Custom Royal convertibles were built. Dodge did break down options by percentage, so experts have been able to estimate that five cars were optioned with the D-500 engine in the Custom Royal series with the manual transmission, but Brown doesn't believe any of those other cars still exist — if they were built at all.

"I have never seen another one, but it would be fun if somebody did come up with one," Brown said. "The guy [who ordered this Dodge] had to specifically de-order it to get the manual transmission. He had to say, 'I don't want it made that way.'"

The partners are aware of another black 1957 Dodge Custom Royal D-500 convertible that sold at Mecum's Belvidere auction in Illinois. That car sported a TorqueFlite automatic. Could it have

The owners' perspective:

Virgil Exner's totally new "Swept-Wing Dodges" took the Forward Look even further with the 1957 Dodges, providing one of the most memorable sales years in the Chrysler Corp. division's history. Our example, a top-of-the-line convertible, is equipped with the exceedingly rare D-500 option package comprised of a 325-cubic-inch, 310-hp Super Red Ram Hemi V-8 engine, Carter four-barrel AFB's and a three-on-the-tree manual transmission.

The 1957 Dodge introduced torsion-bar front suspension. It replaced the old coil springs and shocks and proved to be a major performance improvement. The most expensive model in the Custom Royal series was this convertible, which sold for $3,146, plus options. Total Custom Royal convertible production was 2,456 examples.

Very few Custom Royal convertibles were ordered with the special option D-500 Hemi powerplant. Only 5 percent of all 1957 Dodge buyers opted to spend the extra money on performance. Of that, less than 4 percent of the cars were equipped with a three-speed manual transmission. Simple math indicates that only five cars were built with the rarest-of-the-rare, high-performance D-500 Hemi and manual transmission.

"I almost took off the plastic seat covers, but George said, 'No you can't.' The upholstery is probably so mint [underneath]. But that's the way the car was in 1957."

been the first car Harmon turned down?

Collar and Brown have enjoyed researching their car, talking to its original owner and documenting its history. Their curiosity did get the best of them, and they lifted the rear seat in search of the car's build sheet. It was right where it was supposed to be, and it verified everything they suspected — the car was a true D-500 with a manual transmission.

Though Brown favors restored cars, he and Collar are working to keep their 1957 Dodge as original as possible.

"I almost took off the plastic seat covers, but George said, 'No you can't.' The upholstery is probably so mint [underneath]. But that's the way the car was in 1957."

"We actually prefer finding restored car. The unfortunate part is that we can't find them. But this Dodge is a real cream puff.

"At least half of the [dozen] cars we own have been restored. Especially with these rare old Chryslers, you usually can't get them in any condition, so you have to buy them as you find them."

Brown and Collar favor Mopars, but they enjoy many marques and have found 1950s Chrysler Corp. products to be especially challenging to restore.

"Take 1957, for example," Brown said. "It's a landmark year. Go look at a Pontiac in 1957. They are great cars, and people talk about how rare they are. Then you go look at a 1957 De Soto Adventurer convertible, and they only made 300 of them. If one is offered to you, you have to take it in any condition.

"There is another problem with finned Mopar convertibles that people don't think of — there are no parts for them. I guess my advice to people is don't restore finned Mopar cars. There are lots and lots of Chrysler cars of this era where production is less than 1,000 cars."

Brown joked that he doesn't follow his own advice.

Perhaps it's because he just likes the challenge. Fortunately, with the Dodge he and Collar now own, the most challenging part was convincing the original owner it was going to a good home.

Story by Angelo Van Bogart
Photos by Rick Labuda

ONE GREAT '58

Only 51 years and 22,000 miles keep this 1958 Impala from being new

Chevrolet's first year for the Impala was 1958, and it was offered as the top-of-the-line convertible or two-door hardtop (pictured), in the top Bel Air series. However, the Impala and Bel Air bodies are very different from the cowl rearward.

**Rick Labuda remains impressed with his unrestored
1958 Impala's three-tone upholstery and its design.**

Rick Labuda of Statesville, N.C., never met L.A. Edwards of Crawfordville, Ga., but were Edwards still alive, the two could have been great friends. Labuda is a true southern gentleman, addressing his peers as "sir" and "mister," with a kind, respectful drawl. The cleanliness of Labuda's garage shows a similar respect for the cars it houses, including the still-spectacular, 22,659-mile 1958 Impala Sport Coupe that Edwards bought new, and clearly worked hard at keeping that way.

"This is not a '20-footer,'" Labuda said. "It looks good from two feet away or right on top of it. It's just that nice…with only a few small imperfections."

Since purchasing the 1958 Impala in 2007, Labuda has had a chance to carefully examine the Impala in detail, and he remains as impressed with the factory-sprayed and shimmering Rio Red and Arctic White paint, lustrous 1958 chrome and tight multicolor upholstery today as the day he bought the car. But he nearly missed the chance to own this time capsule.

In September 2007, Labuda was prepared to purchase a low-mileage, original 1956 Oldsmobile Super 88 Holiday coupe that shared an address at Morrison Motor Co. of Concord, N.C., with the 1958 Impala.

**Only a careful cleaning was undertaken inside the Impala.
The two-spoke steering wheel with a chrome ring is an Impala-only unit.**

Since he already owns a 1959 Impala Sport Coupe, and the Olds was priced lower than the '58 Impala, he opted for the Rocket. It was perhaps then that the spirit of L.A. Edwards stepped in.

"I was originally looking at a 1956 Olds, (that was) all original as well, and the Impala. At the time, because of price, I elected to go with the Olds," Labuda said of his decision. "On the day Mr. Morrison was going to deliver the Olds, he called me to say that the Bendix (master cylinder) failed and he was going to order another one. At this point, I felt someone was telling me to go with the Impala. So Jimmy Morrison delivered the Impala instead."

Labuda was thrilled at the chance to be the next caretaker of Edwards' 1958 Impala, and set out to learn as much about the car as he could.

He discovered that, at a time well before anyone purchased a new car with the expectation it would become collectible, L.A. Edwards walked into his local Chevrolet dealership and purchased the Rio Red Impala Sport Coupe as a new car. Alice Thornton, the niece Edwards and his wife raised like a daughter, filled in the rest of the history. She said her uncle loved the Impala and seldom drove it, and when he did, it was to church

and local functions. She said the car was garaged and received plenty of care. Then Edwards' other love intervened and he and the Impala parted.

"In 1975, (Edwards) wanted to please his wife, so he reluctantly traded his beloved Impala for a new 1975 Chevrolet Caprice," Labuda said. "Within one week, he returned to the dealership to repurchase his 1958 Impala, because his wife was not pleased with their new Caprice, only to find that the dealership now wanted twice the amount they gave him in trade. He wasn't able to do it. Within the next week, the car was purchased by a collector, whom I understand

was Mr. Benny Bootle, 1995 president of the Antique Automobile Club of America and a collector of automobiles."

How Edwards' Impala was optioned is nearly as unique as the car's past. The Impala packs the biggest engine offering from 1958 – the 348-cid V-8 with a trio of two-barrel carburetors – all backed by a Turboglide automatic transmission. Other options on the car include a padded instrument panel ($16) and two-tone Rio Red and Arctic White paint ($32), while accessories on the car include fender skirts, a radio and faux exhaust ports behind the skirts. However, the car does not have power steering or power brakes.

Labuda doesn't know the history of his 1958 Impala between Bootle's ownership and when Morrison Motor Co. purchased it with five other collector cars, but he has had a chance to get to know the car itself. He removed the back seat and found a tag installed by the factory that is still in excellent condition, and he removed the headlamp bezels to find that the paint and trim remains as new.

"When I pulled the rear seat out and I saw that tag from the factory still hanging from it, it blew my mind," Labuda said. "The stainless under that seat cushion all looked brand new. Mr. Edwards took good care of it,

and so did everyone else through the years."

Jimmy Patrum and other friends in the Carolina Crossroads Region of the Vintage Chevrolet Club of America (VCCA) inspected the Impala after it was displayed in Labuda's garage and confirmed the car's paint is original, as are its trim, interior and engine compartment.

To keep the car safe and operational, it has received new tires and battery, among other incidentals. The weatherstripping and chrome and other parts remain as they were installed by the factory.

After going over the car with his friends, Labuda decided to enter the Chevrolet in

"The '58 is almost like driving a new car, it's just that comfortable."

the Antique Automobile Club of America's Spring Charlotte meet in the Historic Preservation of Original Features (HPOF) class of judging.

"Before the show, I got a Meguiar's kit with soft soap and wiped it down," Labuda said of the exterior. "I then polished it to get some contaminants off of it and that's it. I just hand polished it – I didn't use a machine." The Impala's spear-shaped side trim was also polished, but Labuda took care not to remove the slightly worn black paint in the trim's recesses. He also polished the chrome bumpers, which are well-integrated into the adjacent sheet metal, making the car's overall design harmonize.

"On the interior, there are some signs of patina, so I didn't try to get rid of that. I just went over the interior with a light cleaning with leather cleaner. I have not shampooed the carpet, just cleaned it," he said.

On April 4, 2009, his work paid off and AACA judges awarded the car HPOF status at the Charlotte meet.

Despite owning a wonderful example of a 1958 Chevrolet Impala, Labuda still has a soft spot for his 1959 Impala Sport Coupe.

"The '59 is a car I'll keep forever," he said.

"The '59 Chevy really appeals to me, because I convinced my dad, who was a MoPar man, to go to the Chevy garage when they first came out and he bought one. When I got married, we used his car. My dad's was a 283 with a Turboglide. This one is a 348 and three two-barrels with Powerglide."

Although Labuda's 1959 Chevrolet Impala Sport Coupe is a relatively original driver with one repaint and more miles than the '58, he's in a unique position to offer comparisons between the two very differently styled and appointed cars, whose drivetrains and X-frames are remarkably similar.

"The '58 is almost like driving a new car, it's just that comfortable," he said. "It has the original shocks on it, but it's a smooth-riding car...the ride is great.

"Both of the transmissions are great, but the Powerglide (in the 1959) shifts faster and the Turboglide (in the 1958) is just very smooth."

Beyond the identical engines and similar chassis construction, Labuda thinks the 1958 Impala is a slightly better car than the 1959.

"What a change between the two model years," he said. "The '58 has so much more quality in the trim inside and on the exterior. To me, it just didn't justify the price increase on the '59 models.

"There's so much stainless steel in the interior, and there's a rear center arm rest in the 1958. The construction of the doors

Labuda also owns this 1959 Impala Sport Coupe, which he and his wife use for touring.

and the interior door panels, what they did with those, there was so much imagination with the 1958. The rear deck, behind the rear window, that's metal. There's stainless around the rear seat backs.

"I would say the '58 is a better car," Labuda adds, noting the panel fit, particularly on the deck lid, is better on the 1958 Impala than his 1959.

After the long and low 1957 Chrysler and Ford models came out, the all-new 1958 Chevrolets were ready for production, and were given General Motors' standard length of time to be engineered and tested after Harley Earl's team designed them.

To catch up with the styling of its competitors after 1957, GM was forced to design entirely new 1959s, which left the 1958 GM models with their own one-year styling cycle, and the 1959s with a shorter length of time before they could be ready for the market. The "Slimline" design of the 1959s is considered a knockout today, even if the cars have a few shortcomings.

For Labuda, both are great cars, and he would be hard-pressed to part with either Impala. Fortunately, Labuda's wife feels the same way, and won't put him in the same position as his 1958 Impala's original owner.

"Yeah, she loves them — all of them."

Story and photos by Angelo Van Bogart

DELIGHTFUL DEPENDABLE DE SOTO

Galen and Fay Erb's original, 110,000-mile 1959 Adventurer has been a family member since '61

Fay Erb purchased this 1959 De Soto Adventurer two-door hardtop as a used car in 1961, then she and her eventual husband used the car daily and through many trips into the early 1970s. The car remains original, down to the black paint.

Galen Erb probably never thought he'd still be with the love of his life and the 1959 De Soto Adventurer two-door hardtop she drove when they were dating, but luck has been on his side. Even luckier, his wife and the car remain as good as they were when Galen met them in 1961.

It was Erb's wife, Fay, who bought the car at the urging of her MoPar-favoring father, but over the past 48 years, it's become her and her husband's family vehicle, if not a family member. The Adventurer's place in the Erb clan was solidified through more than a decade of daily use, which ended shortly after a chance stop at a gas station. There, an attendant started Erb thinking

about the car's future.

"In 1971, I was pulling a little boat trailer when we stopped for gas and the guy wouldn't put gas in it," Erb said. "He said, 'You're not supposed to have that car out.'" Like the Erbs, the attendant was a MoPar fan, and his words hit home. Shortly after the chance meeting, the Erbs parked the Adventurer for 13 years.

Before it began its well-deserved rest in 1972, the fine original car had earned its name and was still looking good. The car was used on such adventures as the Erbs' honeymoon in the early 1960s, which took them from Pennsylvania through Tennessee, New Mexico, Colorado and up Pikes Peak.

"People ask me what it was like at Pikes Peak [with this car] — it was nothing — the car would do it," Erb said.

On another experience, Erb was able to test the dual-carbureted De Soto's power against a carload of kids in a new GM luxury car.

"In 1972, a brand-new Cadillac and two young guys passed and waved, so I let them get ahead of me and guess what — I waved as I passed by them!" Erb said.

On a second trip to the West Coast, the Adventurer was taken across the Golden Gate Bridge and Hoover Dam, driven through Utah and cruised through a giant Wawona tree at Yosemite National Park. Visitors to the The Sands Hotel and Casino in Las Vegas were also treated to a view of the De Soto during the couple's 1968 tour.

After its 13-year-long storage period, the adventuresome De Soto was dusted off and readied for new travels. The thoroughly original car was shown at the nearby 1987 Antique Automobile Club of America's

After 110,000 careful miles, all aspects of the interior remain original, including the gold-and-white vinyl and the shimmering black-and-gold inserts which bring the Adventurer's gold, white and black exterior theme inside. The gizmo atop the instrument panel is the sensor for the automatic headlight beam changer.

1987 Eastern Division Fall National Meet at Hershey, Pa., where it received a First Junior award in a class filled with restored automobiles. Twenty-one years later, the car was on the AACA show field again and shooting for a Senior Award, still with its original interior, black paint and chrome.

After the 1987 showing at Hershey, the Erbs grew even more adventuresome and brought the De Soto all the way to Carlsbad, Calif., for the 1988 National De Soto Club Convention. Twenty-three more trips to De Soto Club Conventions followed, and only rarely were those miles crossed with the Adventurer on a trailer.

De Soto's adventure in greatness

Beginning in 1956, the Adventurer crowned the De Soto lineup in much the same way the 300 capped Chrysler's offerings in 1955. De Soto initially used the name for a concept coupe built inhouse and first shown in 1954. In 1955, another De Soto Adventurer concept coupe bowed, this time called the Adventurer II and built by Ghia

Only Adventurer models feature this emblem on the rear fin, set against a gold-anodized, machine-turned trim panel. The unique gold-coned Adventurer wheel covers also feature gold in the recesses for a very custom look.

in Turin, Italy. The Adventurer name was finally allowed to grace a production hardtop model midway through the 1956 model year. All 1956 Adventurers were two-door hardtops, and all were extensively sprinkled with gold trim, inside and out — a theme that continued through 1959. All 1956 Adventurers were powered by the Chrysler Corp. division's most powerful Hemi, the 341.1-cid V-8 with dual Carter four-barrels helping produce 320 hp.

For 1957, the top-of-the-line Adventurer series gained a convertible model. It also gained taller fins on a new body, as well as a larger engine displacement and higher horsepower rating. The numbers showed 345 cubic inches and a matching horsepower rating for 1957. Through 1959, the Adventurer's performance peak, the displacement and horsepower ratings continued to rise until a zenith rating of 350 hp and 383 cid in the last year of the nifty '50s. That year, the Adventurer retained a dual-carburetor setup and high-lift camshaft, but reached the 350 hp rating with the 383-cid V-8. De Soto copyrighters said the engine provided "'velvet-gloved' might and flashing response."

This De Soto is car No. 510 of 590 Adventurer hardtops built in 1959. With only 97 convertible Adventurers built that year, the hardtop bested convertible sales more than six to one. This car is so original, it retains its OEM wheel chock in the trunk.

By 1959, rumors of 30-year-old De Soto marque's demise were devastating to sales. As the top-of-the-line model, the Adventurer actually did better than its De Soto siblings. Sales of hardtop models were up to 590 in 1959, a sizeable increase from 350 in 1958, and 97 convertible models were sold in 1959, up from an incredibly low 82 convertibles in the recession year of 1958.

Adventurers were only painted pearl white or black in 1959. As an original car, the Erbs' shiny black hardtop still wears flatter black paint with a simulated Scotch-grain pattern on its roof to replicate a leather top.

"The car was built on the morning of March 25, 1959, and first titled in August '59," said Erb. "A young man in his 40s bought it. He had it until April or May 1961."

Since the beginning of the model line, Adventurer unveilings were stalled until months after the debut of the lower-rung Fireflite, Firedome and Firesweep models.

According to Erb, the family's Adventurer was sold new by Brubaker Motors in Lancaster, Pa., a Chrysler-De Soto dealer still operating and the source for a fair number of top-of-the-line Adventurer sales in 1959.

"The dealership sold six or eight of these

[Adventurers]," he said. Erb also noted that a sister convertible built later the same day as his car still exists in Minnesota.

Adventurer convertibles and hardtops are truly sisters. In addition to sharing the same powerplant, all Adventurers feature an anodized gold finish on the grille and on wide, engine-turned side trim running the length of the car. Adventurers also featured exclusive use of stainless trim running around both front and rear wheel openings, joined by a third piece running the length of the 126-inch wheelbase, De Soto's longest. Brightly finished strips on the deck lid were standard equipment on Adventurer, as were power brakes, whitewall tires, backup lamps, power steering and the TorqueFlite automatic transmission. The Erbs' car is further fitted with a triad of horns, an automatic headlight beam changer, six-way power seats, signal-seeking radio with twin rear antennae and a rear window defroster.

Fay finds fate

When Fay and her father spotted the De Soto in 1961, the two-year-old car was parked on a different lot in the same town.

"Fay bought it from Lancaster Sales, a used car lot," Galen said.

"That's the car I wanted," she said.

It must have been the car Galen wanted, too, because from the beginning, he began stashing parts to keep the next-to-new De Soto looking as though it had just come off

Brubaker Motors' showroom in 1959.

"Whenever a part was available, I bought it," Erb said. "When it came to '59 De Sotos, that was my weakness."

Among the parts Galen purchased decades ago was unique gold-speckled black Adventurer carpet and the black-and-gold fabric insert material for the gold-and-white vinyl seats. He's kept the car in great shape and never had to use the spare parts, but retains them "just in case."

Erb says his secret to maintaining the car to its high level for 48 years is largely common sense. "I don't leave the car out of my sight," he said. The car also enjoys heated storage, which has helped ward off the effects of Pennsylvania's climate.

After 23 De Soto club conventions, several trips to the West Coast, adventures to Bonneville to watch Studebakers race and a tour through Glacier National Park, among numerous other destinations, the 110,000-mile, all-original De Soto still looks new and provides its owners with miles of smiles. On its adventures, the De Soto continues to not only please its owners, but those who spot it on its travels.

"It's been a pleasure owning this thing," Erb said. "I get thumbs up!"

Story by Angelo Van Bogart
Photos by Kris Kandler

CATCHING RAYS IN A MONTEREY

Nearly every mile of this 1959 Mercury Monterey's 26,000 has been documented since new

Although its named after a coastal California city, this 1959 Mercury Monterey was built in Metuchen, N.J., one of four Ford Motor Co. plants that built Mercurys that year. The other plants were located in California, Michigan and Missouri.

At its 20th anniversary in 1959, Mercury advertised its latest cars were "planned for people." And over the past 50 years, a small group of people have planned their pleasure around one of those Mercurys — a 1959 Montclair convertible — and accrued only 26,000 miles while doing so.

On June 16, 1959, Mrs. Donna Haigh Budd of Manhasset, N.Y., hopped in her 1955 Mercury coupe and drove to Port Motors, her local Lincoln-Mercury dealership. No one knows if Budd's stop was a service appointment for her 1955 Mercury or if she planned to order a new car, but before she

Advertising actually played down the 1959 Mercury's dramatic tail-end design with wedge-shaped tail lamps. Instead, rear view shots highlighted the Mercury's wide-opening deck lid.

"I parked it in my barn — it has a wooden floor — and kept it covered."

left that day, Budd placed an order for a new Monterey Model 76A convertible coupe in yellow. The car was Mercury's most price-conscious model for top-down fun and had a base price of $3,149.50 before she added options such as an automatic transmission, power steering and brakes, heater and de-froster, radio, padded instrument panel, whitewall tires, back-up lamps, full wheel covers and windshield washer for a grand total of $3,908.45.

On July 1, 1959, Budd left her '55 Merc coupe at the dealer as a trade-in and drove off in her new yellow Mercury. But before she dropped the top of the new Mercury, Budd took out a pen and a new notebook and began recording anything that happened to the car, noting practically everything but the number of dead bugs she cleaned off the grille.

"She kept a little log book, and anytime she went out of town, she logged it," said current owner George Collar. "The car came with every receipt for a grease job, oil change, battery maintenance. We have never seen a better documented car than this particular car."

Beneath the green air cleaner of the 1959 Mercury's 312-cid V-8 was a new Econ-O-Miser two-venturi carburetor "designed to satisfy full power demands, with a special booster that gives finer control of fuel metering" to increase efficiency and save gas. Mercury touted that this engine did not need premium fuel, so owners could "'ride free' 10 miles out of every 100."

As finned MoPar collectors, Collar and his partner Bob Brown have seen many documented original and finely restored cars, but none of them carries this kind of history.

"Besides the original window sticker, we have the original sales contract," Collar said. "We have the original finance contract. She kept track of every mile she drove; her longest trip was to Washington, D.C. — she lived in Manhasset, N.Y., on Long Island."

In addition, Budd also recorded the number of gallons of fuel added to the Mercury's tank and the date of each fill-up. Along with the rest of the Mercury's documenta-tion, Collar and Brown can retrace nearly every mile Budd drove the Mercury until 1977, when the data abruptly ends in Budd's log books. About that time, the car came up for sale at the Antique Automobile Club of America's Eastern Division National Fall Meet at Hershey, Pa.

"That car really stood tall, even at Hershey," said Harland Rusch, of Green Bay, Wis., who was attending the swap meet with his brother-in-law, who lives in Florida. Within two hours of spotting the yellow Mercury Monterey convertible, Rusch and his brother-in-law decided to go 50-50 on the car.

Mercury touted its cars as having the largest windshield in the world. Note how the compound-curved windshield bends over the passenger compartment at the top and extends down to the low cowl, which was a Ford Motor Co. feature into the 1960s. By 1959, the push-buttons were gone from Mercury's new instrument panel that put all of the controls immediately before the driver in a separate pod. This car's original gold-and-white upholstery complements the yellow exterior.

"When I saw that out there, I said, 'That's pretty unique,'" Rusch recalled. He and his brother had the Mercury hauled from the meet in Hershey to Wisconsin, where the car's pampered existence continued.

"I parked it in my barn — it has a wooden floor — and kept it covered," Rusch said. "I started the engine every once in a while. You don't want it to sit eternally; you want oil in the pistons. I think I took it to a couple parades, but I was too worried people would crawl on it. Because of the low-mileage, I didn't want to drive it much."

About 30 years later, Rusch walked in to Larry Fisette's business, De Pere Auto, and offered to sell Fisette a vintage Standard Oil thermometer. Fisette, who makes a hobby of tracking down old iron, knows how to sniff out treasure (he's responsible for finding the "huge muscle car stash" featured in Old Cars Weekly). Fisette asked Rusch if he also had any old cars. Rusch did; in fact, he had four, including the 1959 Mercury convertible.

"He [also had] a 1975 Olds convertible with 18,000 miles on it, a Buick Riviera and he had a 1967 Chrysler," Fisette said. "All

Convertibles are notorious for their lack of trunk space, but not in the 1959 Mercury. This trunk features a six-foot span of clear load area that was easier to reach and use than other cars of the period.

"My first new car was a Mercury, so I've always liked Mercurys."

were rust-free cars, all [were] very, very nice and all stored in a barn.

"I waited for a while and told him I wanted the Merc, but I had to buy the Olds first, then the Buick." Eventually, Fisette was able to buy the Mercury and the Chrysler. Once the cars were in Fisette's possession, he grew even more impressed with their condition.

"He went out there to the barn and he kept the gas tanks up," Fisette said. "I never

had to pull the gas tanks and carburetors to get them to start. He went out there every once in a while and threw Heet in them. Every one of them started up on his [old] gas. I do that now."

While he is a car collector, Fisette is really a matchmaker who enjoys the hunt of finding cars, then pairing them with owners. When he purchased the Mercury, he knew the perfect home for it: the garage of MoPar collectors Collar and Brown. Even though

Mercury's tailfin was straight out of the future. The jet-inspired rear featured a concave area with a convex ridge running through it, capped by wedge-shaped "Buck Rogers" tail lamps.

most of the cars in the partners' collection are De Sotos and Chryslers, Fisette could not have been more right.

"When I was in high school and I was getting my first car, I happened to find a low-mileage 1967 Cougar, and it was a beautiful local car," Collar said. "It was an amazing car even though it wasn't new — I just loved it."

Before Collar was drawn to the Cougar, and the 1959 Monterey convertible much later, Mercurys were a part of his family tree.

"My dad drove a 1964 Mercury Montclair Breezeway sedan," Collar said. "Then my first new car was a Mercury, so I've always liked Mercurys. It's kind of an 'off-brand' car; in succeeding cars I've had a succession of Mercurys."

When Fisette called Collar and Brown about his Mercury find in late 2007, the collectors couldn't resist checking out the car.

"The color and mileage really piqued our attention," Collar said. "He told us about the car right away, and I have always been partial to Mercs. When we heard the mileage, we went over there right away and bought it."

After Collar and Brown agreed to the deal, Fisette's team of experts dove into the car to

"I drive it way too much. I probably drive it once or twice a week, and I know I should not be driving it so much, but I can't keep my hands off it."

ensure that it was road-worthy.

"It didn't take a lot of massaging to get it up," Fisette said. "We did a good cosmetic restoration — whatever it needed. We went through the brakes, and I did rebuild the carb to ensure that it would work for them."

Although the low-mileage Mercury was completely rust-free and showed signs of great care over its nearly 50 years, it had enough paint chips and scratches to warrant extensive paint work to its exterior. The convertible top, passenger compartment (including the interior upholstery) and trunk compartment, however, remain as the Mercury-Edsel-Lincoln division of Ford Motor Co. installed them.

"We ended up rechroming both bumpers, because the back bumper had damage to the chrome from the exhaust," Collar said. "After we rechromed the back bumper, the front bumper looked bad, so we rechromed it, too."

Now that the Mercury is fresh-looking, Collar can't get enough time behind the wheel.

"I can't keep my hands off it," Collar said. "I drive it way too much. I probably drive it once or twice a week, and I know I

should not be driving it so much, but I can't keep my hands off it. It drives so nicely — it starts with the turn of a key and rides so nice, because it's been properly cared for all of its life. I don't put lots of miles on it, but I will drive it to the park or to someone's house or go for a cruise."

Like Rusch, Collar has noticed the Mercury's crisp metal lines are a magnet for attention.

"I stay off the main streets, because it's such a sharp car, it draws too much attention," Collar said. "I don't want people running into me."

Although he avoids endangering the car around John Q. Public, Collar makes sure Mercury enthusiasts get to see the ragtop Monterey. It has been to the Iola Old Car Show and the Meadow Brook Concours d'Elegance, where it participated in a special display of cars from 1959.

Story update

In late 2009, George Collar sold the 1959 Mercury to the grandson of the original owner, who was persistent in his requests to purchase the car from Collar.

Story and photos by Charles E. Marousek

MISS META'S BUICK

It took nearly 20 long years for a Buick admirer to secure a 13,000-mile 1964 LeSabre

The author's pristine 1964 LeSabre has never seen rain in its 45 years. A new set of tires is one of the few things on the car that has changed since the day it left the showroom.

Miss Meta was widowed in 1945 without children and remained a very independent woman throughout her life. Before her husband died, she worked at the Pfister Hotel in Milwaukee Wis., working her way up to head cashier in the "English Room" before becoming its head bookkeeper by the end of her career.

Nearing retirement after almost 30 years at the Pfister Hotel, she decided to purchase a new Buick. On June 25, 1964, she bought a stunning Desert Beige LeSabre four-door hardtop from Lou Ehlers Buick. The LeSabre carried a window sticker price of $3,864.64 prior to the "authorized discount."

Since Meta rode a bus from her apartment to work, the Buick was not used, except for the very occasional trip to her new home being built in Plymouth, Wis. After her retirement, the Buick moved to Meta's garage at her new house.

The years went by, and in 1979, my family had Thanksgiving dinner at my aunt and uncle's home just down the street from Meta. After dinner, my aunt made a plate of food and asked if I would take it to the elderly neighbor lady, and, knowing about her Buick, I jumped at the chance. It was not until 1980 that Meta allowed me in to look at the car. When I finally did see it, the car was covered in blankets and had approxi-mately 9,000 miles on the odometer. When I told Meta that she sure kept the Buick nicely washed and polished, she replied that it had only been washed twice in 16 years and had never ever been in the rain.

Meta died the following year, and it took some time to settle her estate. Meta's nephew, Jim, eventually inherited the Buick, and on Nov. 14, 1984, the title was put in his name. By this time, I was old enough to drive and was keenly aware of the Buick, which I wanted to own someday, so I approached Jim to see if the car was for sale. Jim was polite and always willing to show

me the Buick, but he didn't want to sell it. It sat in his garage while his daily car sat outside.

As the years past by, I made it an annual event to see Jim and ask the same question about the Buick's availability. Unfortunately, the answer was also the same. Jim rarely drove the car, taking it only to an Elkhart Lake golf course about once a summer. Several summers ago, Jim asked if I wanted to drive the Buick, and of course, I said "Yes." It was like driving a brand-new car. On our drive, I watched the odometer turn to 12,500 miles.

The following year, he told me of a flat tire on the Buick, and that the spare finally came out of the trunk for the first time. Shortly after that, new tires were installed and the original spare went back into the trunk.

In 2007, I didn't see Jim for our annual visit. When I returned in 2008, he met me at the door and asked, "Where were you last year?" Again, we made small talk, but this year, the conversation was different. Jim told me he had hit a milestone age and he needed to buy a riding lawn mower. He joked that his car could sit out in the drive-

way, but didn't think the mower should, so he finally offered to sell me the car.

We negotiated a price and a deal was struck. We talked about how fussy Meta had been, and Jim said no one had ever sat in the LeSabre's backseat until he got the car. I told him of my first meeting with Meta and how she explained the car had never been in the rain. Jim said he had never let the car see rain, either. It's probably the only 45-year-old car around that has never seen rain. The miles are accurate and the care genuine.

Before leaving, I asked Jim, "What do we do next year?" He laughed and we shook hands on Sept. 27, 2008, and I proudly backed my new Buick onto the street, noting the mileage of 13,790. On the way home, the Buick made one of the longest trips of its lifetime, from Plymouth to Oshkosh, Wis., (about 50 miles) and performed flawlessly. It remains a true joy to drive.

Story and photos by Angelo Van Bogart

THE CURE FOR...
CORVETTE FEVER

After selling their '61 Corvette, Henry and Naomi Rehfeldt
bought a new '64 Sting Ray — and never let it go

Henry and Naomi Rehfeldt photo

**Henry and Naomi Rehfeldt bought this 1964 Corvette Sting Ray new in June 1964. Thanks to
their appreciation for the car, it remains thoroughly original. The Ford truck also pictured in
this August 1964 photo was a hot rod that Henry built.**

Henry and Naomi Rehfeldt are no
strangers to great cars. Since the
1950s, the couple have built and owned
hot Ford hot rods, cool Chevy customs and
several sweet stockers. Those cars have
since been sold to make room for others,
but it's the 1961 Chevrolet Corvette that
Henry Rehfeldt misses the most.

Henry and Naomi Rehfeldt photo

Beginning in 1964 and through '67, the Sting Ray rear window was a one-piece unit. The slotted wheel covers give the impression of a wheel, thanks to the three-bar spinners. The three-spoke steering wheel and double-hump instrument panel as are Chevrolet installed them. Between the humps is the clock and the car's second-most expensive option, the AM/FM radio, priced at $176.50.

The 327-cid V-8 in this Corvette puts out 300 horsepower; 250 hp was standard, and 365- and 375-hp versions of the 327-cid V-8 were also available. The owner added the aluminum valve covers decades ago, but has kept the painted valve covers that came on the car.

"That's the one I should have kept," Rehfeldt said. "They didn't make many of those dual-quad [cars]."

Perhaps it's the loss of that 1961 Corvette that led the Rehfeldts to buy their second Corvette, a 1964 Sting Ray, from the showroom floor, then never let it go.

"We bought the car on June 24, 1964, from Bob Miller Chevrolet-Oldsmobile in Princeton, Wis., while en route to Wisconsin Dells," he said. "As we drove through Princeton in our black 1964 Chevrolet Impala SS, we saw the Corvette parked in front of the dealership. We went down the road a mile or two when I looked at my wife; she looked at me, and with that look in her eyes, we made a U-turn and went back to look at the car."

The Silver Blue color of the Corvette may have caught the couple's eyes, but it was the car's options that clinched the deal. The St. Louis-built Corvette was was equipped with a four-speed transmission ($188.30), the 300-hp 327-cid V-8 ($53.80), Positraction rear axle ($43.05), 6.70 x 15 four-ply white sidewall tires ($31.85) and a push-button AM/FM radio ($176.40). On top of the Corvette's $4,252 base price, the options added about $500 for a total of $4,804.50, after the $59 destination charge.

The mudflaps have helped keep the original paint on this Corvette in immaculate shape, particularly behind the wheel openings in the body. This car is one of 8,304 Corvette coupes built in 1964 (13,925 convertibles were also built that year). The Silver Blue color of this Corvette was somewhat popular; 3,121 were painted this way.

It didn't take long for a deal to be struck for the Sting Ray, and when the Rehfeldts returned to their Impala to continue their vacation, the owner of the dealership told them to finish the trip in their new Corvette. "I don't know if we just looked trustworthy or if the 1964 Impala we left with him did the trick!" Rehfeldt said.

Since the black Impala SS was a trade-in, the Corvette was the Rehfeldt's only mode of transportation for a period. Naomi used the car for her daily commute to work, but made sure to park it away from other cars to avoid dings and dents in the sharp creases of the Corvette's fiberglass body. To keep the car out of rough Wisconsin winters, the Rehfeldts eventually purchased a second vehicle.

1964 was the second year in a Corvette styling cycle that began in 1963 — a year which marked the first time in Corvette history that a fixed-head coupe was added alongside an open-top model in the Corvette line. For the first Corvette Sport Coupe, Bill Mitchell's design team integrated a split rear window in the fastback, which allowed the ridge started in the roof to extend down the rear of the car. This "spine" was just one design feature that mimicked the graceful sea creature for which the car was named. In emulating the stingray, the General Mo-

"People are impressed by the car's originality, especially the carpet."

tors design team blended round curves with sharp creases in all the right places to make the new Corvette harmonize with the road and strike a chord with driving enthusiasts.

Only one year later, the split was removed from the rear window and the backlight was made as a one-piece unit. Even though most collectors today seek the 1963 "split windows," many new Corvette buyers were glad to see the one-piece rear window; some 1963 owners even removed the section of body that split the rear window into two pieces to install 1964-and-later rear windows. Because of today's preference for 1963 Sting Ray, Rehfeldt has noticed very little attention is given to 1964-and-later models.

"'64s are in the shadow of '63 Corvettes," he said. "You don't see or hear about too many '64s."

The Rehfeldt's 1964 Corvette sports only 42,000 miles, many of which came on the drive from the couple's central Wisconsin home to Chicago and the Twin Cities, as well as two trips to Florida — all in the first 10 years.

Rehfeldt said he didn't expect to own the car this long but, perhaps subconciously, the couple began planning for long-term ownership many years ago. Rehfeldt purchased a new exhaust system (still wearing the price tags) and tail lamps from the dealership and has since replaced the mufflers, but he never had a need to install the replacement tail lamps. In fact, the car remains in largely original condition, down to the paint, interior and mechanical components, including the all-important, numbers-matching engine, transmission and rear end.

"People are impressed by the car's originality, especially the carpet," Rehfeldt said. Among the impressed are appraisers, at least one of whom has commented that the paint is the nicest he has seen. Rehfeldt is also quick to point out the seams that hold the Corvette's fiberglass panels are visible through the 45-year-old metallic paint.

The car remains very authentic, but Rehfeldt did install aluminum Corvette valve covers shortly after buying it new.

"I thought, 'Why would GM put those tin valve covers on a car with all of those other aluminum parts?'" he said. But the Corvette purists need not to worry — Rehfeldt has the still-mint orange originals hanging from his garage wall, complete with runs in the paint as applied from the factory.

These days, the Rehfeldts' Corvette is driven only to shows. Its daily-driver days are far behind it, and the Rehfeldts don't seem anxious to make the same Corvette mistake again.

Story and photos by Angelo Van Bogart

YENKO SURVIVOR
OUTRAN THE BUTCHERS

Since his Yenko/SC Chevelle is a little battered and bruised, Chad Blomberg decided to treat the street eater to a full body-off-frame restoration that will be completed in the summer of 2004.

To restore or not to restore? The answer was simple for Chad Blomberg when it came to his 18,000-mile 1969 Yenko/SC Chevelle. This steroid-pumped dealer muscle machine will be restored.

The Chevelle's original LeMans Blue paint will be stripped, as will the yellowed Yenko stripes that were carefully applied by Don Yenko's daughter 35 years ago at a reasonable $5-a-car fee. But in place of the weather-checked original blue hue will lie

a show-quality coat of LeMans Blue paint with fresh, bright white Yenko graphics to be applied by well-known muscle car restorer Roy P. Mastel (RPM) of RPM Restorations. And the result will be suitable for a car as rare as this Yenko/SC Chevelle.

As good as this Yenko/SC Chevelle looks, the accompanying photos hide some of the blemishes it has gathered during its 35-year lifetime, despite the fact that many of those years were spent in storage. Blom-

Don Yenko's daughter charged him $5 for each Super Car she striped.
This Chevelle still wore her handiwork before its restoration.

berg found the 427-cid-powered Chevelle in the hands of a noted Yenko expert who had purchased the car from the original owner in 1989.

The Yenko's first owner lived in Pennsylvania, the home state of Don Yenko and his Canonsburg, Pa., Chevrolet dealership. Yenko hopped up several Chevrolet models, including Camaros, Corvairs, and a few Corvettes. Yenko also tricked out 99 1969 Chevelles, like the one pictured here, through Yenko Sports Car, Inc., a division of his Chevrolet dealership. The 427-cid Chevelles he sold with Yenko/SC stripes were fit with mighty big-block engines by

Chevrolet under Central Office Production Order (COPO) 9562 at the Tonawanda, N.Y., plant.

After taking delivery of this Chevelle from Yenko's dealership, the original owner drove it sparingly around Pennsylvania avenues until he parked it in the early 1980s.

More importantly, the first owner of this Yenko/SC Chevelle left his car completely untouched, which is what attracted Blomberg to this particular Yenko. As was the case with many muscle cars, most Yenko/SC Chevelle owners pulled off the exhaust manifolds in favor of headers, removed the emissions equipment, and slapped on dif-

"They [Yenko cars] got raced hard and beat to hell. You never find a Yenko Chevelle in this condition."

This patriotic red, white, and blue Yenko emblem has only seen 18,000 miles pass by.

Gone but not forgotten, traces of the original "sYc" markings still remain on the headrests.

Many Yenko owners cut the back part of the Yenko/SC graphics off of their cars.

The original Yenko/SC 427 sticker still clings to the radiator support.

ferent carburetors and manifolds to take advantage of the already-potent 427-cid V-8's gobs of power, which Yenko rated at 450 hp (Chevrolet stated it was good for 425 hp). But not this Yenko Chevelle. It still had all of its original parts, down to the A.I.R. pump, exhaust manifolds, and carburetor. It even had the original tires on it when Blomberg

bought it, although they were too cracked to be road-worthy.

"[Other Yenko owners] blew up motors and they blew trannies," he said. "They [Yenko cars] got raced hard and beat to hell. You never find a Yenko Chevelle in this condition."

Such abuses to these high-performance

It ain't pretty, but it's all here, from the original exhaust manifolds to the A.I.R. pump. Few muscle cars can make such a claim.

Chevelles have left only 37 known survivors, and of those, Blomberg said only a few have their original engines, let alone other original mechanical components.

"Everything original to this car is still on it," he said.

"The doors close like a new car, and the door panels aren't warped like they usually are," RPM said. RPM has started restoring the Chevelle for Blomberg and knows a low-mileage muscle car when he sees one, having owned and restored several Chevelles and numerous other performance cars of all persuasions in his 20-plus years in the restoration business. His plans are to give the original interior only a thorough cleaning.

Father Time and storage had wreaked havoc on other aspects of the virginal car, causing Blomberg to favor a body-off restoration after acquiring the car in the summer of 2002.

"The paint was kind of checked and cracked, and there were some rust holes in the bottoms of the fenders," he said. "It just wasn't quality enough to leave alone."

Before getting the restoration started, however, Bloomberg had a chance to drive

it around his Minnesota town.

"It ran out very well for being the original motor, as a typical 18,000-mile car would," he said. "It still felt very tight, performance and steering-wise."

Blomberg even hit a few local shows after acquiring his Chevelle, but because of its lack of SS emblems and its patina, most people walked right by the car without no-ticing it. Others wrongfully assumed it was a clone.

When its restoration is completed, the Yenko Chevelle will be in good company with Blomberg's 1970 Chevelle LS-6 SS454, a 1970 Dick-Harrell Camaro, and a Yenko Deuce Nova that he recently acquired.

Story by Angelo Van Bogart

RACER X

Restorer's unrestored LS6 race car remains a bit of a mystery

This LS6 1970 Chevelle SS454 was raced until it had about 700 miles. Roy and Cindy Mastel recently bought it with 800 miles and now have 1,000 on the odometer.

They say the shoe maker goes without shoes, and the same could be said for muscle car restorer Roy P. Mastel and his wife Cindy.

The couple have long restored all types of muscle cars, but have a personal preference for 1970 Chevrolet Chevelle SS454s. In fact, it was a Cranberry Red 1970 SS454 LS6 sport coupe that helped Mastel start his restoration business in the early 1980s.

After friends saw his work in reviving the derelict Chevelle, they suggested he restore cars for others. The Chevelle was sold and RPM Restorations (named after Roy's initials) of Minnesota was born.

In the intervening years, the Mastels have purchased several unrestored 1970 Chevelle SS454 LS6s to restore for themselves, but it seems a customer always spots the cars and winds up buying them.

"Everything was really nice, except the rear quarters were cut for bigger tires."

And even when one of the Mastels' personal Chevelles finally nears completion, it's sold before it's completed and the search for another starts again.

One of the Mastels' recent Chevelle finds is a particularly interesting car — an 800-mile, ex-drag car with many original features. "Everything was really nice, except the rear quarters were cut for bigger tires, so I put new GM quarter panels I've had since the 1980s on it," Roy said. After replacing the quarter panels, Mastel painted them with white primer to match the remaining original paint. Aside from the quarter panels, only the doors have ever been repainted, but there's a good reason for that.

"They took the paint off the doors to remove the name before [the racers] sold it," Roy said. Luckily, removing the car's racing name from the doors didn't wipe away its past. (More on that later.)

For racing, the car was further modified with a full-race Turbo Hydra-Matic 400 using the original transmission. The car also has a higher stall converter and came with 4.88 gears, which Roy since replaced with stock 3.31 gears for driveability. Mastel also removed the car's roll bar and put on an exhaust system to make the old quarter-mile warrior highway friendly. New rubber was mounted on the car's period Fenton drag wheels. Unfortunately, the original block is long gone, an expected casualty from a tough life running full-bore, 1,320 feet at a time. Judging by the numbers in the block, the replacement LS6 engine block was installed around 1975.

True to a purpose-bred race machine, the Chevelle doesn't sport many options.

"It didn't come with a console. It's a bench seat car with an automatic on the column," Roy said. "The only options it really had was a Cowl Induction hood with the SS stripes and tinted glass. They didn't order any gauges since they bought aftermarket parts."

The car does have the standard-for-SS454 power disc brakes, but the Chevelle didn't come with power steering and is radio delete. "It's the only time I have ever seen a '70 Chevelle with a radio delete plate," Mastel said.

The Mastels don't know a lot of the details of the car's track history. They knew the LS6 was raced out of central Louisiana and was purchased new alongside an LS6 convertible that was also raced through a dealership in that area.

"It only had 700 miles from racing," Roy said. "Cindy figured out how many runs that

"You don't really cruise in this car — it's more of a pounder. I pound on this car because I don't have to worry about chipping paint and scratches."

is down the quarter-mile." (It's about 1,400 runs, assuming all of the miles were accrued going down the quarter-mile and back.)

The Mastels bought the car from a friend, who pried the Chevelle loose from someone in Louisiana who didn't want to part with the car's old racing photos plastered on his walls and other documentation. The Mastels hoped they could find physical evidence of the car's history in other ways. That chance came after the car was pictured in *Old Cars Guide to Auto Restoration*. There, a reader recognized the car, thanks to its unique combination of sponsor stickers, its low miles and its original location.

"[We found out] Bill Robinson from Houma, Louisiana, owned the car," Cindy Mastel said after a conversation with Robinson. "Bill bought it from Marv Bourg, who raced it out of Trap Chevrolet. "It was called 'Lil Hanky' after Hanky Trap's son, owner of the dealership."

The Chevelle ran like a bat out of hell, proven by quarter-mile times in the 10.90-second range in A/Stock-Automatic at Southland Dragway in Louisiana. (Period road tests put performance for an automatic-equipped LS6 with a 3.77 rear axle in the 13.8-second range.) The stresses of racing in the 10-second area also explain why the LS6's original engine is long gone.

"I asked him about the original engine, and he said that 'It blowed it up when it was new,'" Roy said.

The Mastels also learned the LS6 convertible that was originally purchased and raced with their Classic White sport coupe was Fathom Blue with white interior and was called "Tinker Toy." A race car hauler was used to tow both LS6 Chevelles to the track, and it still exists, too. Meanwhile, the convertible has since been restored.

While Roy and Cindy Mastel continue tracing the car's history, they're having fun driving their old race car.

"You don't really cruise in this car — it's more of a pounder," Roy said. "I pound on this car because I don't have to worry about chipping paint and scratches."

Story by Angelo Van Bogart
Photos by Bill Dorst

THE WORLD'S BEST HEMI?

One owner and 1,800 miles make this '71 Challenger among the finest

Greg Hernandez walked into his local Iowa Dodge dealership in late 1970 and ordered this Hemi Challenger R/T. In all the years he's owned it, Hernandez has only put a little more than 1,800 miles on the car, and today, it remains an unrestored original.

Some might think owning a Hemi Challenger R/T since new and putting only 1,800 miles on it is like buying a *Playboy* magazine and never getting to the centerfold. But that's exactly what Greg Hernandez did, and today, he has what might be the nicest original and lowest-mile 1971 Hemi Challenger R/T in existence.

At the age of 29, the railroad employ-ee and family man marched into Hendryx Motor Co. in Centerpoint, Iowa, on October 19, 1970, and ordered himself a 1971 Challenger R/T. The car was built Saturday, Nov. 7, 1970, and was waiting on the lot for Hernandez by Dec. 8 of that year. Hernandez drove down to the dealership on a cold, December day, laid the keys to his 440-cid-powered 1969 Dodge Charger on the sales-

The last time most of the bolts holding this car together were turned was before it rolled out the Hamtramck, Michigan, assembly plant on November 7, 1970. That's how untouched Hernandez' car is. Those vents behind the doors are unique to 1971 Challenger R/Ts, as are the longitudinal stripes.

man's desk, and walked out with a Hemi-powered machine. And then the Challenger R/T sat. And sat.

"It was December in Iowa, and it was snowy," Hernandez recalled. "To begin with, the Hemi Challenger was hard to start in the winter, and I had to commute 40 miles to work and could not see driving that nice car to work every day." Plus, "the car is useless in the winter." Driving to his job site through the debris-riddled rail yard also posed a problem when it came to keeping the car in nice shape, so to get to work, Hernandez bought a new VW Beetle for commuting, and used it for many years. "I drove the wheels off that VW," he said.

Thanks to the VW, the Challenger R/T was reserved for nice days when Hernandez didn't have to work, a rare occurrence in it-self. At the same time, Hernandez was rais-ing a family, and since he worked weekends and holidays, the car rarely saw the road, aside from the occasional jaunt around the block or to the store. The farthest the Hemi Challenger R/T traveled was from Hernan-dez' driveway to the dealership where the car was purchased.

But why trade in a two-year-old 440-cid-powered Charger for a Hemi Challenger R/T? Hernandez explained that after read-ing in hot rod magazines that 1971 was the last year a Hemi engine would be available,

After hearing the 426-cid, 425-hp Hemi engine would not be available after the 1971 model year, Hernandez rushed out and placed his order for a Hemi Challenger R/T hardtop equipped with the powerful (and pricey, at $789.85) optional engine.

he wasn't going to let the opportunity pass him by. Hernandez' only roadblock to his Hemi dream was at the dealership.

"The gentleman who sold me the car had only sold one other Hemi car, and he had a big problem with it," Hernandez said. "The gentleman [who bought the Hemi car] came back with a broken engine only months after he got it. The dealership replaced the engine, and pretty soon, he came back with another broken motor, but they didn't replace it. The salesman wasn't enthused about me buying the car with the Hemi, but I said, 'I definitely want it.'"

When he placed his order for the Challenger R/T, he checked the boxes for the A833 four-speed transmission (D21), Super Track Pak (A34), power brakes (B51), console (C16), bucket seats (C55), Sport hood with "426 Hemi" nameplates (J54), and black longitudinal R/T sport stripes (V6X) on an unusual coat of Dark Gold Metallic paint (Y9) with a full gold vinyl roof (V1Y).

"I heard someone mention that it's such a gentleman's color; I agree with that," Hernandez said. "It's something that you love or hate. I didn't know too much about the Hi-Impact Colors at the time, and the salesman showed me little [paint] chips, and I thought, 'That looks like a great color.'" Hernandez has displayed the car at the Mopar Nationals

Dodge Challengers received a major restyling for 1970, so for 1971, only minor changes were carried out. These chiefly included a new grille and rear panel treatment with 1971-only taillights.

in Columbus, and he reported that the unrestored Challenger's color received many compliments.

"Everybody just loves the color," he said. "It's unusual to see one of these cars in this color. A lot of people thank me for saving the car; it's pretty nice of them."

Since only 71 Hemi Challenger R/T hardtops were built, they are exceedingly rare, especially with such low mileage. And unlike most other extremely low-mileage, ultra-muscle cars, this untouched Challenger never saw a "Christmas tree" at a local race track, or even a street race. Heck, few

people ever knew Hernandez owned the car, because it was out so seldomly. Only his neighbors knew there was a beast lurking in the garage.

"Right after I bought it, I replaced the exhaust and put on headers and header mufflers," he said. Occasionally, Hernandez would fire up the car to "keep things moving." During the Challenger's early days, the Hemi's boisterous exhales through the headers could be heard by neighbors all around. Since then, appreciating the car's collectible status, Hernandez has replaced the headers with the original manifolds and has fit

Hernandez did it right: That Pistol-Grip shifter tops off an A833 four-speed manual transmission that transmits power from the Hemi engine to the rear end. The gauge cluster includes a tachometer. When all was said and done, the car carried a $4,862.35 price tag, a considerable increase over the $3,252.00 Challenger R/T base price.

reproduction mufflers. He could have even put the original exhaust system on, but he tucked it under his mobile home, and when he moved some years back into a house, he forgot to take the parts with him. Hernandez tried to go back for the parts, but the mobile home had been bulldozed and the parts were long gone.

At the same time he installed the headers, Hernandez fit the Challenger with a set of aftermarket Ansen mag wheels that he had run on the Charger he traded in. The tires rubbed the Challenger's fenders, so Hernandez put the original steel wheels and Polyglas GT tires back on the car.

As a kid growing up in Texas, Hernandez was heavily influenced by the car culture there, and he attributes his purchase of the Hemi Challenger R/T to the automotive lifestyle he loved. He considers his low-mileage and completely unrestored car to be representative of that legacy.

Now that Hernandez is retired, he has time to enjoy his nearly 35-year-old purchase. The Challenger sees many more miles, though from an enclosed trailer that takes it to Mopar events throughout the country.

Story and photos by John Gunnell

HEMI IN HIDING

After 35-year slumber, rare Hemi Challenger is a show stopper

This 1971 Dodge Hemi Challenger Mr. Norm's GSS hardtop has a 116-inch wheelbase and tips the scale at 4,140 lbs. With white stripes on a red finish, the car is an eye-catching Dodge. It has a black vinyl interior and optional wood-grain steering wheel.

When Mike and Ivy Guarise go shopping for a car, they aren't likely to worry about clunker programs — or even gas mileage. Their 1971 Challenger is far from an economy car with its 426-cid/425-hp engine, four-speed transmission and Super Track Pack rear axle. The car doesn't clunk, but it could clobber lots of its street racing rivals in the Traffic Light Grand Prix.

Dodge had scored a hit with its first pony car, the 1970 Challenger. Up until then, Chrysler's "white hat" division had relied on special versions of the mid-size Charger and Coronet to please anyone wanting big muscle. Those who preferred pint-sized performance had some hot editions of the compact Dart to chose from. The Challenger was something

It is thought to be among the most original, most documented, lowest-mileage Hemi Challengers in existence.

else and won immediate acclaim.

With the Plymouth Barracuda due for a total restyling in 1970, Mopar management finally handed Dodge the same package. This allowed it to create a truly sporty compact car with a 2 + 2 configuration that allowed it to compete head-to-head with Pontiac's Firebird and Mercury's Cougar.

The Challenger succeeded so well that it outsold the Barracuda in its first year. The muscular Dodge racked up 83,000 units of production versus 55,000 for Plymouth's "fish" car. The next season, though, sales fell off drastically and the Challenger sold just 30,000 units. That's not the only thing that makes Mike and Ivy's car a rarity, however. Their Challenger was purchased as a new car from Chicago's high-performance king, Mr. Norm of Grand Spaulding Dodge. It is one of approximately 12 Hemi Challengers made with the same drive train and the desirable "shaker" hood.

With the Challenger, Dodge was clearly selling performance in a package that looked the part. It's not surprising that 93 percent of the 1971 model run was fitted with V-8 engines, even though the "slant six" was available. Nearly 17 percent were optional engines, ranging all the way up to the 425-hp Hemi that is under the hood of

the Guarises' car.

From a historical perspective, 1971 turned out to be the last year for the 426-cid Hemi as a factory option. New emissions standard, safety rules and insurance considerations put the horsepower race under a caution flag in 1972. However, in 1971, Dodge was definitely promoting power and performance and Mr. Norm was happy to stir in some of his own ingredients.

The Street Hemi engine, a $790 option on the '71 Challenger, had continued basically unchanged after its introduction in 1966. It had a bore and stroke of 4.25 x 3.75 inches, a 10.25:1 compression ratio, hydraulic valve lifters and dual four-barrel Carter AFB carbs mounted inline.

On the Hemi Challengers, a flat-black finished air scoop was mounted to the carbs and poked through a hole in the hood. The impressive "shaker" hood was so named because you could watch the torque twist the engine as throttle was applied. Some cars also had chrome NASCAR-style hood hold-down pins.

The original owner of the Guarises' car elected to have Mr. Norm replace the shaker hood with a lightweight fiberglass hood. The legendary tweaker was then asked to bolt on a set of headers and add his Stage III

"Dynotuned" engine upgrades.

As indicated by the R/T initials at the tail ends of the white body stripes, the car has Dodge's "Road & Track" high-performance goodies. The R/T package for the '71 Challenger included Rallye suspension, an instrument cluster with an 8,000-rpm tachometer and 150-mph speedometer, plus heavy-duty drum brakes, chrome exhaust tips and distinctive graphic stripes.

Other extras included twin outside rearview mirrors and an AM/FM/cassette stereo with rear speakers and a microphone.

After a summer of terrorizing the streets of Madison, Wis., in 1971, this car was sold to a friend of the original owner. The new owner had realized that it was a rare piece and decided to preserve it. The car was coated in WD-40 and put into storage, and it remained in hibernation for the next 35 years.

In 2006, the car was taken out of storage and Mopar historian Galen Govier was contacted to inspect the vehicle and document its history. The Challenger was covered with dust, but turned out to be a remarkably well-preserved car.

Now, it is thought to be among the most original, most documented, lowest-mileage Hemi Challengers in existence.

Story and photos by John Gunnell

CORVETTE CAPSULE

Rare '72 Corvette ZR-1 Survivor is 290 miles from new

Finished in white with a tan leather interior, the 1972 Corvette ZR-1 is a subtle-looking piece of automotive history until you lift the hood and spot the LT-1 engine.

Former Corvette designer Al Wagner of Delafield, Wis., is an expert on the C3 Corvettes made from 1969 until 1981. The only thing Wagner didn't know about these cars was how perfect Guy Carpenter, of Marshfield, Wis., had kept his rare 1972 Corvette ZR-1 for 37 years.

"When Guy came up to me and said that he had a car I might be interested in, he was kind of messing with me," Wagner recalled. Carpenter had bought the car new to preserve it, and that's what he did!

The ZR-1 — one of just 20 made in 1972 — was never dealer prepped or titled. Carpenter purchased the car new on Feb. 12, 1972, in Rockford, Ill., and then trailered

Wearing its original air cleaner element, the high-performance LT-1 small-block V-8 even has its original Goodyear fan belt.

it home with help from his brother. They had to get permits from both Illinois and Wisconsin to transport an unregistered car. From that time on, it was driven only 290 miles, mostly in one-mile trips around the block. These trips were made chiefly to circulate the fluids a few times each year.

Each time the car was driven, the seats were covered with towels and the driver removed his shoes and drove in his stocking feet. The Corvette was never driven on its original wheels and tires. A second set of wheels and tires was swapped for the originals each time the car was used. The original tires are weather-cracked, but otherwise look like new and have factory stickers on them.

The antifreeze in the car was never changed until Wagner got it. He was careful to change it without removing any clamps or hoses, to avoid compromising the car's originality. The car has had an oil change and the battery has been replaced by a reproduction made by Antique Auto Battery of Ohio. The battery is mounted behind the driver's seat and still has the factory-installed hoses that were designed to vent acid gases to the atmosphere.

"I have owned so many 1972 Corvettes and I never saw the hoses on any car before," Wagner said.

The tan leather seats still have a new-car smell. The packet on the driver's side floor contains some of the mountain of documentation Al Wagner received with the car.

The car was stored in Marshfield, Wis. in a regular garage with a concrete floor and no heat.

"There was more aging than I would have expected, because they didn't put it in a museum," Wagner said. Other observers might argue that there is absolutely minimal aging of any type on the vehicle. Wagner plans only to clean it and leave everything as is.

The body of the Corvette has no wear and tear of any kind. The black underside of the hood is one of the telltale places that show just how pristine the car is.

"Look how the white shows through the black," Wagner pointed out. "Even cleaned-up Survivor cars usually have the paint touched up and you never see white showing through on them. The car has factory over-spray in a few under-car areas, and you can see places where the factory workers touched painted parts together and left remnants of the paint on the touched parts. The car has all of its factory markings, dots and paint marks."

Under the hood, where the matching-numbers, high-performance 350-cid/255-hp V-8 engine sits, you notice that the car still has its original air cleaner element. Naturally, it is dirty from years of sitting, but not from driving. You might also notice

Although the needle "parks" over one of the numbers, it's clear that the speedometer reading inside the Corvette is low. It stands at 290 miles.

what looks like tape partially scraped off by the radiator.

"That is actually the backing from a piece of foam that was stuck on the radiator shroud of most '72 Corvettes," Wagner explained. "The ZR-1 did not have a radiator shroud, but a factory worker must have stuck it on and then tried to remove it."

Inside, the car's saddle tan leather interior has no scratches or flaws. You can still smell the leather seats. The carpets, which were usually covered, are like new as well.

"Look at the car — really, it's a noth-

ing-looking car with its white body and tan seats, but remember, it's a racing car," Wagner said. Guy Carpenter did some racing at the time and only racers were allowed to plan an order. Even with his racing credentials and the fact he was a Chevrolet salesman, his first order for a ZR-1 was rejected. That's why he went to Lou Backrodt Chevrolet in Rockford to finally get the car.

Only 65 Corvettes with the ZR option were produced in the '70s, with 25 ZR-1s built in 1970. In 1972, production was eight ZR-1s and 12 ZR-2s. The last 20 made in

"Of the 20 made in 1972, 10 are known to still exist. But you never know what will show up in the future — like this car."

Special heavy-duty brakes have pins to help hold the calipers together.

1972 were all ZR-1s. The ZRs had the "special-purpose" LT-1 V-8 and were not available with power windows, power steering, air conditioning, a rear defroster, wheel covers or a radio. They included a close-ratio four-speed gear box, heavy-duty power brakes, an aluminum radiator, special springs and shocks, a front stabilizer bar and rear wheel spindle strut shafts. The option was priced at $1,010.05.

Wagner does not claim the car to be the lowest-mile ZR-1. He said it is the car with the lowest known miles.

"Of the 20 made in 1972, 10 are known to still exist," Wagner said. "But you never know what will show up in the future — like this car."

According to Wagner, all of the original paperwork for the car was given to him when he purchased the Corvette.

"This has been Guy's car all along for all those years, and that's what it states on all the paperwork," Wagner said. "His brother helped him maintain it, because he was a mechanical type of guy. They were very respectful of the car and took care of their stuff. No guy but Guy would have done this so well."

Wagner said he feels the car is priceless and he doesn't plan to sell it. "Guy didn't want it blown out in the marketplace or going to an auction that was a circus," he said. "He wanted someone who can appreciate the car and take it to the right forums."

Story by Angelo Van Bogart
Photos by Mike Sylvester

GOT SOME SPEED?

Mr. Norm's Demon GSS does

Mike and Victoria Sylvester's Mr. Norm's-prepared 1972 Dodge Demon GSS is one of 50 or 51 built and one of 6 or 7 survivors with the original engine. It's painted High-Impact Hemi Orange (EV2) with a black vinyl top, the black stripe kit on the sides and hood, and has an original factory hood scoop.

G ot Some Speed? "GSS" may not be an acronym for that question, but it is a question that Mike and Victoria Sylvester can answer "Yes" to with their unrestored, supercharger-spinning 1972 Dodge Demon GSS (Grand Spaulding Sport) built courtesy of Mopar performance idol "Mr. Norm" Kraus.

The Chicago dealer, famous for adding extra bite to Dodge products through his Grand Spaulding Dodge dealership in the muscle car era, waved his magic crankshaft on the Sylvesters' Demon and 49 or 50 others to answer performance needs in a time of decreasing compression ratios and stringent emissions standards. Mr. Norm's

efforts would close out the muscle car era. Thanks to him, it went out with a blast.

Sylvester's GSS hails from the second year Mr. Norm built the potent model in his dealership. The first 1971 models packed the already-brutal small-block 340-cid V-8, but Mr. Norm replaced the four-barrel carburetor and manifold with a six-pack set-up to raise the horsepower from 275 to 290.

When the 340 V-8's compression dove from 10.0:1 in 1971 to 8.5:1 in 1972, Mr. Norm had to get serious in order to maintain the performance prowess of his GSS. In years of researching his high school dream car, Sylvester learned that's when Mr. Norm hooked up with the folks at Paxton.

In 1971, Mr. Norm met with Paxton representatives, and from their meeting, a supercharger kit was made for the small-block Mopar engine. A test kit was installed on a 383-cid-powered Demon (obviously not a factory installation), and the car was driven coast-to-coast through dirt and other less-than-ideal conditions. Afterward, the engine was torn down to prove to Mr. Norm that the Paxton supercharger would not only provide extra power, but was also durable.

Following the test and Mr. Norm's "thumbs up," as Sylvester describes it, Gary Dyer of Grand Spaulding Dodge worked with Paxton to develop the supercharger for the 340-cid V-8 to be equipped in 1972 GSS models, which were available by late 1971.

Mr. Norm advertised the Demon GSS as "the most exciting new high performance car concept on wheels today" in a single-

**Hood stripes covering its dual-snorkel hood scoop
add to the Demon GSS' sinister demeanor.**

column advertisement. The ad also listed the equipment a gearhead could get in his Demon GSS. Performance goodies such as a fresh-air intake and filter unit, oversized pulleys that provided 7 pounds per square inch of boost, a modified fuel pump and fuel pressure regulator, heavy-duty aluminum valve spring retainers, a jetted and calibrated carburetor, and a curved distributor were all advertised as part of this "performance plus package" that left the shop dyno-timed and Sun-scoped. The $3,595 price also included the Sure-Grip rear-end, Wide-Oval "boots," and a heavy-duty TorqueFlite transmission.

The combination of equipment produced an estimated 350-380 hp, according to Sylvester, who revealed other special equipment not included in the ad.

"The '72 had quite a few other mods, including epoxy-coated floats... The stock one would crush under the boost of the supercharger," Sylvester said. "The air filter was located in front of the grille for ram effect... and different pulleys could be bought to increase boost.

"These cars were tested in the Midwest with slicks running high 12s pretty consistently," Sylvester added.

But the fun couldn't last forever, and by late summer 1972, the EPA was on to Mr.

This ad lists the equipment included on the Demon GSS.

Norm and his GSS super cars, Sylvester said. Because of government intervention, there would be no 1973 Demon GSS cars from Mr. Norm.

"At the time, it was illegal for a dealership to perform high-performance modifications. Even though [Mr.] Norm did it under another company name, they were not fooled, and [they] threatened Norm with a fine," Sylvester said.

The Sylvesters' 56,000-mile Demon GSS shares space with a Dodge Avenger raced in Colorado's NASCAR super stock division, a '68 Charger R/T in original condition, a '70 Duster 340, and a modified '69 340 six-pack Dart Swinger. Sylvester also buys, sells, and trades Mopar cars and parts as a hobby.

Sylvester said his GSS remains in "as-found condition, with the exception of a complete tune-up and tuning for [Colorado's] mile-high altitude. The Demon even passed Colorado's very tough emissions standards," he said. "You should have seen the emissions person's face when he was looking at the Paxton supercharger. I believe he just thought it was a huge air conditioner!"

An internet ad led Sylvester to Delphi, Ind., where he purchased the GSS in February 1999. The Hemi Orange 340 Demon already in Sylvester's collection had to be sold in order to fund the GSS, but he "was not about to let this one go by."

After he purchased the GSS, Sylvester directed his research efforts toward the history of his own car. So far, he has turned up three previous owners and other bits about the car's past.

"We do know at one point the car sat outside near a barn for 11 years before being discovered,

Under the hood on this unrestored Demon GSS is a supercharged 340-cid small-block.

[yet the] car is in amazing original condition and does not appear to have ever been raced hard," he said.

Sylvester now stores the GSS in his race shop between showings at local Mopar shows, but he plans to restore the High-Impact Hemi Orange (EV2) car down to its original luster and freshen the engine internals in the process.

Sylvester said many of these cars received smaller pulleys. As a result, the cars suffered engine blow-outs, but his Demon still sports the never-opened original engine. During the restoration, Sylvester will be the first to see the inside of his Demon's

340 since the Chrysler factory workers who put it together more than 30 years ago.

When he does put the GSS engine back together, there will be a few upgrades.

"I'm going to restore it to original GSS standards with a few mods to the internals of the engine," said Sylvester, citing such tweaks as a different camshaft and lightweight pistons and rods. He also plans a mild porting and three-angle valve job to the original heads, along with the installation of an upgraded torque convertor in the transmission with a shift kit.

"Other than that, the car will be in 100-percent as-sold and dealership condition,"

The supercharger in the unrestored engine bay of the Sylvesters' Demon GSS is capped with "Mr. Norm's Supercharged GSS" and produces 7 psi of boost.

Sylvester said.

Currently, Sylvester's GSS is one of two unrestored cars left in existence and one of six or seven 1972 GSS cars left with matching numbers and documentation.

"Our Demon has the original invoice and advance dealer notice to Grand Spaulding Dodge, which shows the car was shipped from the Hamtramck assembly plant to Grand Spaulding Dodge on Feb. 18, 1972, via Cassens Transport," Sylvester said.

Of the six or seven survivors, only one of them, a Bright Blue metallic (B5) car, is equipped with the rarer four-speed transmission.

Sylvester has found that the supercharger gives the GSS steady performance. He is also familiar with the 1971 GSS models and notes, "The 1971 GSS Demon with any of the 340 six packs, if not tuned correctly, is a handful, as 1,190 or so cfm is a lot for a 340. They ran good, but not as good as the larger 440 six-packs."

Because of government intervention, the 1972 GSS was the last of dealer-tuned and built Mopar muscle cars, but thanks to Mr. Norm, the muscle car era ended in Chicago with a tire-screeching cloud of smoke!

By Gregg D. Merksamer
By Angelo Van Bogart

TWO BOATS CROSS PATHS IN PA.

Old Cars contributor, editor find cars near fall meets

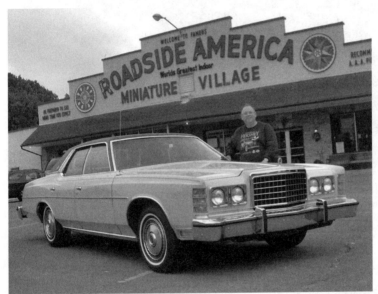

Gregg D. Merksamer poses with his 22,000-mile 1978 Ford LTD outside Roadside America in Shartlesville, Pa., two hours after taking delivery. The car was found during the AACA's National Fall Meet at Hershey.

Old Cars Editor Angelo Van Bogart's 17,000-mile 1981 Impala coupe, which was purchased in Bethlehem, Pa., at the time of the 2006 Fall Carlisle event. It still wears its original tires and the seatbelt instructions are still attached to the passenger's visor!

THE FORD

Constructed during the 75th anniversary of the Ford Motor Co.'s founding in 1903, this 22,080-mile 1978 LTD was the last true full-sized Ford passenger car available before the "downsized" 1979 versions debuted. While it measures 224.1 inches long and 79.5 inches wide, its 4,215-pound curb weight is still at least a half-ton less than a modern Ford Expedition or Chevrolet Suburban. This body style, designated 53H, is officially known as a four-door pillared hardtop for combining frameless door glass with a sedan-style center post.

This particular LTD was registered on March 30, 1978, to Palmyra, Pa., resident Arlene E. Rupp and her husband, Floyd B. Rupp, Sr., who was a service technician at J.C. Hess Ford of Hershey, Pa. Its $5,410 base retail price was boosted to $7,933.10 by several unusual options, including a 400-cid V-8 engine with a two-barrel carburetor for $283. (An even bigger 460-cid four-barrel V-8 was also available for $428.) The car also carries four-wheel disc brakes ($197), a heavy-duty trailer towing package ($139) and for another $49.10, special-order 7080 Pale Jade exterior paint normally used on Ford trucks.

They purchased this car to pull a 24-foot Trotwood trailer, but a 1971 LTD finished in a similar shade of green remained their primary tow vehicle. The 1978 saw little use

before Rupp stopped driving it altogether around 1988.

Having become the service manager at another dealership, Rupp remained extremely diligent about maintenance and kept the car garaged. Even after his death in 2002, the car was still sent regularly to Maguire's Ford in Palmyra, Pa., which had taken over J.C. Hess' franchise, for a current state inspection and any needed servicing.

My opportunity to purchase this LTD arose three months after Arlene Rupp passed away in July 2006. The car was parked alongside Pennsylvania State Highway 39 to attract a buyer from the legions of old car enthusiasts attending the Antique Automobile Club of America's gigantic fall meet in Hershey. The car drove almost like new despite its lack of exercise, and the artifacts that Sherry and John Ebersole (the original owner's step-daughter and son-in-law) included with the sale were astounding! This included two copies of the original build sheet; the original window invoice; the original odometer statement and temporary registration certificate; the original paper key tag with the dealership's stock number; a paper loop of starting and safety belt instructions that slips over the sun visor; a complete set of service manuals; and a license frame, ashtray and leather key fob from J.C. Hess Ford.

I decided to name the car Myra, in honor of the first 28 years it spent residing in Palmyra, Pa. My wife, Lisa, immediately took to calling it the "mint condition car," on ac-

count of its unusual color as much as its remarkable state of preservation.

With Lisa following behind in her Ford Taurus wagon, we put 172 miles on this LTD during the first day we owned it, which was more usage than the car had seen over the previous 8-1/2 years! According to the service records supplied by Maguire's when they replaced the alternator belt at 22,089 miles for our trip home, the car had accumulated just 64 miles since its last oil change in November 2003, 76 miles since the battery was replaced in January 2003, and 89 miles since new tires were fitted in February 2002. In other words, the oil and filter change that we performed once we got home took place 239 miles, or two years and 11 months, after the previous one!

Displayed, for the very first time with just a perfunctory cleaning beforehand, at the Up-per Delaware River Mustang Club's Inaugural Fall Car Show in Montgomery, N.Y., on October 15, 2006, Myra was honored with first place in the 1967-1979 Ford class.

— Gregg D. Merksamer

THE CHEVY

Just one week before *Old Cars Weekly* contributor Gregg D. Merksamer found his low-mileage, single-family-owned 1978 Ford LTD outside the fall AACA event in Hershey, Pa., I was finalizing the deal to buy a 17,000-mile, one-owner 1981 Chevrolet Impala coupe from Bethlehem, Pa. And neither of us knew about the other's find.

It's hard to explain, but I love full-size Chevrolets from the 1980s, and I have since they first came out. My first Caprice was a 1982 coupe, and the most recent was the 1985 Caprice Classic Landau coupe I still

Old Cars Auction and Technical Editor Ron Kowalke helps load the Impala
for its trip home to Wisconsin.

own. Though I've owned the 1985 Caprice coupe for five years, its Landau vinyl top treatment never grew on me. I've always considered the full-size 1980s Chevrolets to be extensions of the Bel Air and Biscayne two-door sedans from the 1960s, and the vinyl top masked that look.

Not content with the Landau top and extraneous trim on my 1985 Caprice, I joked with *Old Cars Weekly* staffers that if a nice 1980-'81 Impala coupe without a vinyl top came up for sale, I'd consider buying it. Not two weeks later, I had to put my money where my mouth was or stop talking.

Upon finding the Impala listed for sale,

I contacted the Bethlehem, Pa., seller from my Wisconsin home. It turns out that he is a salesman at a Volkswagen dealership. One of his customers drove a VW Jetta, but her husband owned a Chevrolet truck and 1981 Impala coupe. For 25 years, her Jetta had been parked outside next to the truck while her husband's Impala sat in the garage, rarely gathering miles. When she bought a newer VW, she told her husband she had enough — her VW was going in the one-car garage.

I have to credit her husband with getting away with preserving the Impala for 25 years. Judging by the never-used snow tires

and tire chains in the trunk, the car was probably intended to be daily transportation, or maybe that's how he justified its purchase. But day after day, the Impala quietly sat in the garage while the couple used their VW and truck to commute to work. According to the seller, the Impala's owners only drove the car to prevent its tires from weather cracking. Otherwise, it sat in the garage.

Why anyone would preserve a 1981 Impala since it was new is a question that baffles even a 1980s Chevrolet collector like me. Perhaps the owner decided to keep the car for special occasions when he learned that Impala coupe sales were so bad in 1981 — only 6,067 were built — that the model was cancelled for 1982.

Regardless, the owner couldn't bear to allow the car to sit outside, and when he shared the Impala's outdoor plight with the VW salesman, the salesman offered to buy the car.

It turns out the Impala's original owner thought that the salesman would be the Impala's next preservationist. Instead, the VW salesman did what he did best — he turned the car around and offered it for sale as soon as the new title arrived.

The car was a 1981 Impala coupe built at the Oshawa, Ontario, assembly plant and sold new through Scott Chevrolet of Emmaus, Pa., on May 23, 1981. The original owner traded a 1974 Buick Regal coupe after finding the Light Blue Metallic Impala with 10 miles on the odometer sitting on the new car lot.

Options on the car do not include a V-8 engine, which was priced at only $50 more than the V-6 model. Oddly enough, the fac-

tory deemed it necessary to include bumper guards at $54, however. The original window sticker states the car also sports air conditioning, tinted glass, front and rear floor mats, and an electric rear window defogger, as well as an AM/FM stereo and the value appearance group (wheel opening trim). The total, including tax and fees and the Rusty Jones treatment, was $9,443.50.

Along with keeping the window sticker and new car sales agreement, the owner kept meticulous service records, and judging by the copious notes in the owner's manual, he actually read the manual from cover to cover. He also filled out the maintenance schedule included in the new-car paperwork. The paperwork included a schedule for studded tire usage with Pennsylvania and New York

circled, perhaps offering a clue as to where the owner intended to use the car.

The car was also accompanied by the dealership stock number tag, key knockouts, dealership odometer statement from the time of delivery, original title and the paper seatbelt instructions over the passenger-side visor.

While the Impala is in my possession, chances are nil that the car will ever wear those NOS snow tires and still-packaged tire chains. It may also accumulate its most miles in one trip in a return adventure to Pennsylvania for the Fall Carlisle and Hershey events. Unless I find another low-mileage car to bring back. And Gregg Merksamer doesn't beat me to it!

— Angelo Van Bogart

Story and photos by Sharon Thatcher

OHIO COLLECTOR HAS SHARP EYE FOR ORIGINAL BARGAINS

More than 20 years ago, Dan Varner picked up a 1969 Coronet Super Bee and today the car still has only 59,000 miles. Varner says the only thing not original on the car are the valve cover gaskets.

Some collectors spend years looking to find their dream cars. Dan Varner of Delaware, Ohio, has a different approach: he waits for them to find him. Today, he has a stable of six low-mileage, show-quality cars, and he never actively looked for a single one. Varner is just one of those lucky guys who has also developed a keen sense.

"I can smell an old car in a garage just by walking past," he says.

He developed that sense by buying and selling cars as a hobby. "Once, I bought a convertible, a 1966 LaSabre, for $600 and sold it for $900 and I was tickled," he said. He had other sales throughout the years, owning up to 11 cars at one time. But not

"This one only survived because it had older first-owners."

until his 1964 Impala came along in 1980 did he start to collect them. Like the first car he ever owned (a 1960 Chevy Impala two-door hardtop), the '64 is white with red interior. He learned that the owner was in a nursing home and needed to sell it. The car was in immaculate condition, with just 27,000 original miles on the odometer, and it was love at first sight. He quickly purchased the car from the owner's financial caretaker.

In 1988 came his 1969 Dodge Super Bee

with 59,000 miles. It had never been advertised; the owner's grandson just knocked on his door one day to tell him about it.

"He said, 'I notice you like old cars,'" Varner recalls the teenager saying, and from there he explained that the car was for sale, and that his grandmother didn't want to advertise it in the newspaper. "She didn't want to have to deal with people coming to look at it."

Varner enjoyed buying and selling nice old cars as a hobby and often had them

"It's all original. Nothing except the valve cover gaskets; they've been replaced, and that's it."

sitting around his yard for sale. "Mostly 1960s," he says. "As a teenager growing up, I just loved the body style. It was a great time to grow up with cars." So, out of curiosity, the next day he called the grandmother. "She didn't know much about the car," Varner says, but in their conversation he learned that it was a 1969 Dodge Coronet with hood scoops and a stripe in back. "That's all I needed to know," he said. "I knew it was a Super Bee".

The Super Bee was Dodge's popu-lar muscle car, first introduced in 1968 to compete against Plymouth's lower-priced muscle car, the Road Runner. It was espe-cially popular with young men anxious for Friday nights to arrive. Most Super Bees were washed and shined for a night cruising to the drive-in for a hamburger and shake, then pranced off to some drag strip of high-way for a tire-burning good time to release some pent-up horse power and hormones. Over time, they were used and abused. Most didn't survive their owner's youth. "95 per-

cent of the demise of cars from that era were owned by young drivers who went out and raced them," Varner says. "This one only survived because it had older first-owners." Grandma's husband was in his 50s when he brought the white Super Bee home from nearby Delaware Dodge.

During their ownership, the car was well cared for and driven sparingly. At the time of Varner's purchase, within 36 hours of getting that fateful knock on the door, the car had 54,000 original miles on the odometer. Rust was non-existent, even in the rust-prone areas of the trunk and engine compartment. It remains that way in Varner's care.

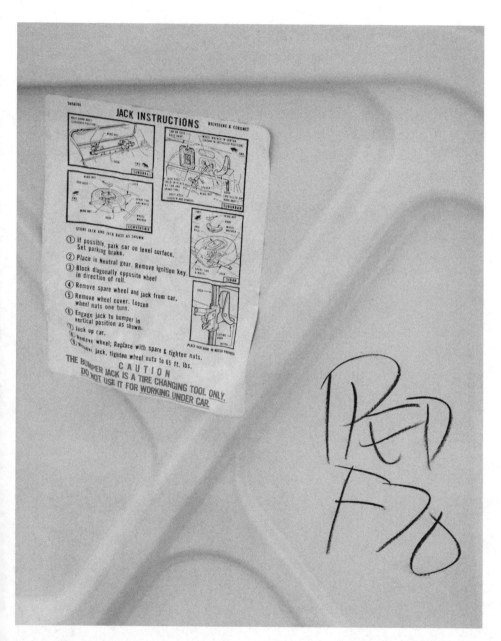

"Nothing has been changed", he points out. "It's all original. Nothing except the valve cover gaskets; they've been replaced, and that's it."

Part of the $4,200 purchase price Varner paid included the original window sticker. It shows that the Super Bee listed for $3,121 plus options for a total of $3,488.60. List-

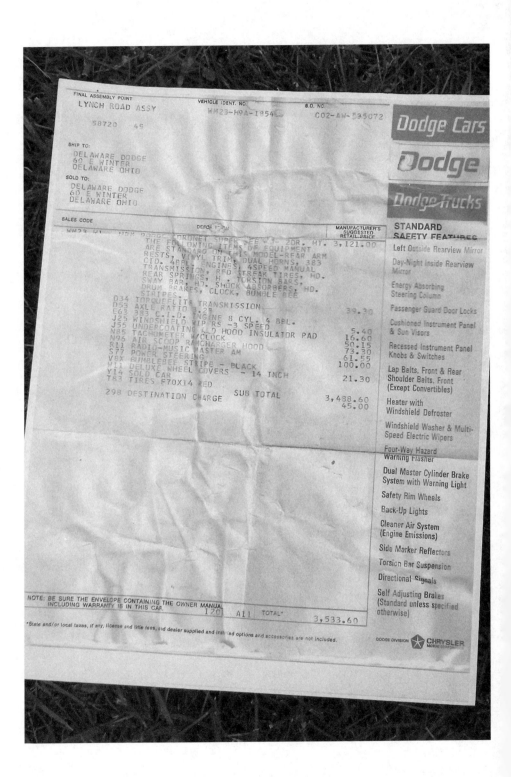

FINAL ASSEMBLY POINT
LYNCH ROAD ASSY

VEHICLE IDENT. NO.
WM23-H9A-195461

B.O. NO.
C02-AW-535072

58720   49

SHIP TO:
DELAWARE DODGE
60 E WINTER
DELAWARE OHIO

SOLD TO:
DELAWARE DODGE
60 E WINTER
DELAWARE OHIO

SALES CODE	DESCRIPTION	MANUFACTURER'S SUGGESTED RETAIL PRICE
WM23 U1	WDR DODGE CORONET SUPER BEE-V- 2DR. HT.	3,121.00
	THE FOLLOWING ITEMS OF EQUIPMENT	
	ARE STANDARD ON THIS MODEL-REAR ARM	
	RESTS, VINYL TRIM, DUAL HORNS, 383	
	CID. 4BBL. ENGINE, 4SPEED MANUAL	
	TRANSMISSION, RED STREAK TIRES, HD.	
	REAR SPRINGS, H. TORSION BARS,	
	SWAY BAR, HD. SHOCK ABSORBERS, HD.	
	DRUM BRAKES, CLOCK, BUMBLE BEE	
	STRIPES.	
D34	TORQUEFLITE TRANSMISSION	39.30
D53	AXLE RATIO 3.23	
E63	383 C.I.D. ENGINE 8 CYL. 4 BBL.	
J25	WINDSHIELD WIP RS -3 SPEED	
J55	UNDERCOATING W/D HOOD INSULATOR PAD	5.40
N85	TACHOMETER W/CLOCK	16.60
N96	AIR SCOOP RAMCHARGER HOOD	50.15
R11	RADIO-MUSIC MASTER AM	73.30
S77	POWER STEERING	61.55
V8X	BUMBLEBEE STRIPE — BLACK	100.00
V11	DELUXE WHEEL COVERS - 14 INCH	
Y14	SOLD CAR	21.30
T83	TIRES F70X14 RED	
	SUB TOTAL	3,488.60
298	DESTINATION CHARGE	45.00

NOTE: BE SURE THE ENVELOPE CONTAINING THE OWNER MANUAL
INCLUDING WARRANTY IS IN THIS CAR.   1201   A11   TOTAL*   3,533.60

*State and/or local taxes, if any, license and title fees, and dealer supplied and installed options and accessories are not included.

Dodge Cars

Dodge

Dodge Trucks

STANDARD SAFETY FEATURES

Left Outside Rearview Mirror

Day-Night Inside Rearview Mirror

Energy Absorbing Steering Column

Passenger Guard Door Locks

Cushioned Instrument Panel & Sun Visors

Recessed Instrument Panel Knobs & Switches

Lap Belts, Front & Rear

Shoulder Belts, Front (Except Convertibles)

Heater with Windshield Defroster

Windshield Washer & Multi-Speed Electric Wipers

Four-Way Hazard Warning Flasher

Dual Master Cylinder Brake System with Warning Light

Safety Rim Wheels

Back-Up Lights

Cleaner Air System (Engine Emissions)

Side Marker Reflectors

Torsion Bar Suspension

Directional Signals

Self Adjusting Brakes (Standard unless specified otherwise)

DODGE DIVISION   CHRYSLER MOTORS CORPORATION

ed as standard was its four-speed manual transmission, rear arm rests, vinyl trim, dual horns, a 383 CID 4 BBL engine, RFD streak tires, heavy duty rear springs, heavy torsion bars, sway bar, heavy duty shock absorbers, heavy duty drum brakes, a clock and its bumblebee stripes.

Extras included a TorqueFlite transmission, 3-speed windshield wipers, undercoating and hood insulator pad, tachometer with clock, air scoop Ramcharger hood, an upgraded Music Master AM radio, power steering, and 14-inch deluxe wheel covers.

The 1969 model varied little from its 1968 predecessor. Added features included the TorqueFlite automatic transmission, a wider bumblebee stripe, a "Scat Pack" badge on the grill and trunk, plus front fender engine call-outs.

Altogether, 27,800 Super Bees were produced in 1969, which included 166 powered with a Street Hemi V-8.

Unlike most of the cars Varner has owned over the years, the Super Bee has not been for sale. It's "a keeper," he says.

In 1995, a 1975 Cadillac Coupe deVille d'Elegance came into his life with 17,000 miles — literally owned by a little old lady who probably only drove it on Sundays. It arrived after a tip from his wife's cousin, who is a car salesman in Van Wert, Ohio.

Next to come along, in 2004, was a 1987

One of Dan Varner's fleet of all-original cars is this 1987 Buick Grand National with only 59,000 miles.

The Grand National's interior is still like new.

"With a restored vehicle, you just don't know what it looked like before it was restored, what was covered up."

Buick Grand National that had seen only 59,000 miles. Like the Cadillac, it came as a tip from his wife's cousin.

And in 2005, his 1987 Buick Regal with just 13,000 miles found him. "It was advertised in the newspaper," Varner recalls. "It was a very cold weekend in winter, it was below zero, and I don't think anyone wanted to go out in the cold to look at it, except some idiot."

But, Varner is no idiot: he has the car.

Varner knows the lineage of each of his vehicles. In all cases he is either the second or third owner, and he knows the names of each proceeding owner. He also knows the dealerships where each of the cars was purchased.

Varner's cars have not been expensive to purchase. Added up, he spent less than $35,000 for his first five. All five have been

The previous owner of this 1975 Cadillac Coupe de Ville
rolled up only 17,000 miles on the odometer.

This 1962 Chevy Impala 409 coupe has just 54,000 miles.

It's a good bet there are few 1987 Buick Regals around with fewer than the 13,000-plus miles that have been registered on this car's odometer.

relative bargains in large part because of their the age and the fact that the hobby is only beginning to show respect for original, untouched vehicles. "If they had a ding or a little bit of fading, judges didn't like that," Varner said. He sees it differently: "With a restored vehicle, you just don't know what it looked like before it was restored, what was covered up; it could have been a rust bucket."

Although his cars have taken a long time to garner respect in the hobby, Varner enjoys traveling to car shows to show them off. "People are just amazed to see them in such original condition," he says. To keep mileage low, he usually attends only local shows, putting only 1,000 to 1,500 miles yearly on all of his cars combined.

It doesn't bother Varner that not many shows offer judging classes for unrestored cars. "I'm not a trophy-prone person," he says. "I don't care about the trophy; I al-

The interior of the 1987 Buick Regal is every bit as pristine as the exterior.

ready own the trophy."

The sixth car in Varner's stable, a 1962 Impala 409 with 54,000 miles, is his most recent purchase. Unlike the others, however, it has seen some restoration, but like the others, it came to him with little effort. "It belonged to a friend and I told him if he wanted to sell it some day to let me know. Two weeks later, he contacted me," he says.

His collection is outgrowing his available garage space, but Varner is not prepared to offer any guarantees on what turn his hobby will take next. Fortunately, his wife Gloria approves. "Everybody has to have a hobby," she says. "He gets a lot of enjoyment out of it. And as I tell people, when we're out together and he does a double take, I know he's not looking at another woman."

See more photos of Varner's collection online at www.oldcarsweekly.com

Story and photos by John Gunnell

ORIGINALS ONLY

Unrestored cars shine at Bloomington Gold event

Ken Kaufman of La Crosse, Wis., owns this 1969-1/2 Trans Am with only 44,800 documented miles. Kaufman believes it may be the lowest-mile example in existance.

On June 28, 2009, the Pheasant Run Resort in St. Charles, Ill., hosted the second annual Bloomington Gold Survivor Collector Car event. About 120 cars were on the show field, and most of the vehicle owners paid a fee to have their vehicles "certified" by a team of judges. The goal was to determine if the originality level of each judged car was within certain estab-lished guidelines. Cars deemed to be within the guidelines were classified several ways.

Bloomington Gold CEO David Bur-roughs decided that the 2009 Survivor Col-lector Car event should recognize several different grades of original vehicles. There-fore, the cars granted certification ranged from perfectly preserved cars in nearly new condition to those appearing tattered, but

This silver-gray Cadillac Coupe deVille would be a winner in anyone's book, whether or not the judges bestowed an award on it. The car was well-preserved and looked absolutely untouched.

too historically important to restore. Burroughs said, "The Survivor Collector Car show will allow owners, restorers, historians, photographers and experts alike to reference the only true sources for authenticity — the cars themselves."

The original Bloomington Gold rules specified that a vehicle must be at least 20 years old, capable of making at least a 20-mile test drive and judged to be more than 50 percent unrestored, yet with finishes, surfaces and overall condition good enough to use as a reference for authentic restoration of a similar vehicle.

Eight new award categories were created for 2009. These categories for unrestored vehicles were broken down into 10-year periods starting with cars and trucks built in 1969 or earlier and extending to vehicles built in 1989 or earlier. Depending on the age, a vehicle could exhibit a limited amount of restoration measured in percentages to receive certain awards.

Among the other interesting awards was "The Forget it. Restore it" award for unrestored, 1979-and-older vehicles that were in original condition, but poorly preserved. With tongue planted firmly in cheek, the Bloomington Gold Web site suggests, "Forget It standards are reserved for cars at least

Nick Januszczak of Hammond, Ind., owns three Indiana-built Studebakers, including this turquoise-colored 1964 Avanti hardtop.

30 years old, mostly unrestored and shot (or at least pathetically ugly)." They had to be capable of driving on the field under their own power, "but smoke is OK. Extra credit for strange clanking noises, rust or nests of small animals. Poor restorations or cars simply beaten with hammers are ineligible for awards."

Lost & Found Awards went to 1969-and-older vehicles never before displayed at a show. These are cars that spent most of their lives in garages, warehouses or barns, but have never before been on public display. Vehicles had to be unrestored, un-refinished, unaltered and have no more than moderate

deterioration to receive an award.

Only original-owner vehicles of 1989 and older vintages could compete for Owner One awards. This designation was also reserved for the original owners of a vehicle who held possession for at least 20 years.

The show announcer clarified that Survivor judging tries to honor the work of the factories that built the vehicles and owners who cared for them over the years, rather than shops that restored them. "These vehicles display the intricacies and fingerprints of their histories, rather than the monotonous shiny paint and chrome of antiseptic show cars," he noted. "They speak in quiet

Texan Jimmy Smith poses with the '69 Pontiac Grand Prix that he recently bought. The car came with plenty of dealer documents.

whispers of credibility, rather than shouts of 'Look at me!'"

Burroughs said he was very happy with the second edition of the new show.

"We have about the same number of cars that went for recognition and certification," he said. "The number of display cars is down because we had to raise the cost to cover higher expenses. Some people decided not to bring their cars, because they didn't want to spend the extra money to park on the fairway." He said that's why some cars were in the general parking area.

"We are mainly interested in people who really understand the importance of having their cars certified," said Burroughs. "So they got a legitimate piece of paper that shows that a group of independent experts has looked at it and put their stamp on it. You will see that over the next year, this will be growing and becoming more important to collectors."

Burroughs estimated that 20 percent of the participants came more than 500 miles to the show. "If we just drew a local crowd with cars that really weren't all that well preserved, I would not be happy; I would say we're missing the mark," he said. "But, when you get people driving 500 miles, across the U.S., to come, it means they trust

Richard Torricelli, of Staten Island, N.Y., brought his 1976 Monte Carlo to the Bloomington Gold Survivor show on his way back from a Western hunting trip.

Automotive writer Andy Mikonis, of Chicago, Ill., recently purchased this well-preserved 1970 Jaguar 4.2L E-Type Series II coupe. He found the car for sale in the Detroit area.

Dan Schmidt, of Cleveland, Ohio, had his 1968 Shelby GT500KR judged by the certification experts. The bright red "pony car" uses a Cobra Jet 428 V-8 for power.

you that well. And they'll trust us more in the future when word gets out about how good these judges are and the kinds of cars we're certifying. This will build more trust in people and I feel really good about that."

The show CEO explained that he had seen the same thing years ago with Corvette certification judging. "It takes a while to figure things out; people don't want to jump into doing things they really don't know about. Once people know what we're doing and tell others they had a nice, enjoyable time and that we are nice people, they'll come here ... People will discover that, if they have a vehicle that's unrestored, they will not get a bigger welcome, anywhere on earth, than they will when they come here."

The next Bloomington Gold is set for June 24-27, 2010, and if the format stands, the non-Corvette Survivor Collector Car show will be on June 27 next year. "We'll be here at Pheasant Run until there's a reason to go elsewhere," said Burroughs.